INSIGHT TO
IMPACT
STRATEGIES FOR INTERPERSONAL AND ORGANIZATIONAL CHANGE

INSIGHT TO
IMPACT
STRATEGIES FOR INTERPERSONAL AND ORGANIZATIONAL CHANGE

William G. Dyer
Brigham Young University

Brigham Young University Press
Provo, Utah

Library of Congress Cataloging in Publication Data
Dyer, William G
  Insight to impact.
  Edition of 1972 published under title: The sensitive manipulator.
  Includes bibliographies.
  1. Leadership. 2. Social interaction. 3. Behavior modification.
4. Organizational change. I. Title.
HM141.D9 1976   301.15'53   75-29146
ISBN 0-8425-0067-7
ISBN 0-8425-0070-7 pbk.

Library of Congress Catalog Card Number: 75-29146
International Standard Book Number: 0-8425-0067-7 (cloth)
                                 0-8425-0070-7 (paper)
Brigham Young University Press, Provo, Utah 84602
1976 5M 11053

CONTENTS

PREFACE

My world is filled with requests from people who want something in their world to change: a wife who would like to change the relationship with her husband, a manager who is dissatisfied with the way he works with his staff, an executive whose goal is to realize greater production and profits, or a teenager who is unhappy at home.

I have been struggling with the issue of planned change for more than twenty years and have attempted to bring together in this volume some of the insights and understandings that I think will help others achieve the changes they desire. This book is an elaborated and revised edition of my earlier work *The Sensitive Manipulator: The Change Agent Who Builds with Others* (Provo, Utah: Brigham Young University Press, 1972). Sixteen chapters from the previous volume have been revised and expanded for this publication, and nine completely new chapters have been added.

This volume is directed to those in the expanding professional world centered on helping and change. These professions include consultants, change agents, organization development specialists, management trainers, personnel specialists, and increasing numbers in education, the ministry, law, social work, and nursing whose work is change-centered. The first nine chapters may help them plan strategies for helping others work through interpersonal problems. These chapters would also be helpful to those seriously planning changes in their life situations. Thus, anyone whose interpersonal world needs alteration will hopefully find a set of strategies to help devise a plan for achieving the impact he desires. Change can be judged successful only if the consequence of the change program is close to the change envisioned at the beginning. The title of this volume, *Insight to Impact,* suggests that change has to be thought about, implemented, and then assessed to see if the impact is the one desired. Anyone concerned with change in his interpersonal world may find some insights that will help him achieve his desired impact.

Chapters 10 through 16 were written to help those interested in changing organizational conditions and in planning and implementing a program of organizational change. For many years I spent a great deal of time in group training — actually trying to bring about individual change through group processes. But my experience was somewhat disheartening. I found that many people who were perceived by themselves and others as significantly changed for the better soon reverted to old behavior when they were plunged back into systems, groups, and organizations that did not support the new behavior I had helped them develop. This led me into the whole field of organizational development — with its emphasis on diagnosing systems, planning changes in basic policies, procedures, task arrangements, rewards, and ongoing relationships that will support and reinforce the insights individuals have. Organizational support is often a necessity if insight is to achieve impact.

Chapters 17 through 20 provide a discussion of a number of common organizational conditions that discourage or oppose change. These barriers can be met and removed if an effective change plan is developed.

Chapters 21 through 25 are written for the professional trainer and consultant, especially those in the process of developing the skills currently deemed important in the field of organizational behavior.

In presenting this volume, I recognize my academic and intellectual heritage. Anyone reading this will see immediately my reliance on such writers as Likert, Argyris, McGregor, Maslow, Rogers, Beckhard, Gibb, and many others. My early training was guided and stimulated during the exciting late fifties and sixties in the National Training Laboratories Institute for Applied Behavioral Science. I am also indebted to many colleagues in many places. My own department at Brigham Young University and my friends there are a great current stimulus. I am also aware of the debt I owe to a series of organizations and managers who have allowed me to work with them and gain the practical experience needed in developing my own ideas about organizational change.

I wish to acknowledge the assistance of Brigham Young University Press, especially Elizabeth P. Thorpe and Michael M. Kawasaki for their work in moving this project along. I would also like to thank Cynthia M. Gardner for copyediting the manuscript and William F. Whitaker for drawing the illustrations.

INTERPERSONAL COMPETENCY

Interpersonal behavior usually begins with one person's initiation of action or interaction toward one or more others to achieve some purpose or goal. At one time a manager may call in an employee to clarify a report or to receive instructions. Later he may want to instruct, stimulate, encourage, or support the same employee. The goal in human interaction is to achieve our intentions.

Intention and Impact

Intentions are the end results or goals we hope to achieve with others as we begin an interaction. Person A has some *intentions* toward B. He wants to encourage, clarify, instruct, or take some action that will be the first step toward the achieving of his goal. Hopefully he will make on B an impact consistent with his intentions.

Behavioral Gap

However, between *intention* and *impact,* the actual effect of one's behavior, are two major gaps that must be considered and to some degree managed. (See diagram of the interpersonal flow.) Person A must translate his intentions into behavior, and for some people most of the time, and others some of the time, this is a major difficulty. The behavior that is expressed may be a very clumsy representation of the intention. If you were to talk with the subordinates of some managers you would find they feel hostile, defensive, and resistant to their boss. A conversation with the boss would disclose he is distressed his workers feel that way, for he certainly did not intend that reaction.

It sometimes occurs that a person has unconscious intentions

1

that are displayed exceptionally well. These are results or impact goals one actually would like to achieve, but since they are often not socially (or personally) acceptable or desirable, we keep them hidden even from ourselves. A manager, for example, may at some deeper level distrust his subordinates, and his behavior communicates his distrust very accurately. At the conscious level he would say that the communication of distrust is not his intention. One of the important reasons for getting feedback is to help the receiver examine, honestly, his total intention system — both conscious and unconscious.

"Filter" System

The point of distortion between intention and impact may also be in the "eye of the beholder." The behavior of A may be a very clear representation of his intentions, but if B has a clogged filter system or perceptual screen and perceives the behavior quite differently than was intended, the resulting impact will not be what A desired. Person B may have a thick antiauthority filter, which causes him to resent anything a superior does. He interprets attempts to clarify or encourage as disapproval or control. All of us have filters; we are aware of some parts of them and blind to others. Our filters are made up of our biases, prejudices, values, experiences, and feelings.

In either event, whether the problem of the undesirable impact results from Gap 1 or Gap 2, the result for A is the same: he has not achieved the consequence he intended.

Competency in Change

Anyone who is concerned about influencing others to make changes in their performance or behavior must take into account the kind of impact he is having on others, particularly those he is asking to make a change. Whether he is a manager or professional change agent, the measure of his competency is the degree to which he is capable of achieving the results he intends with others. The competent person (in this framework) is one who is capable of rather consistently doing so. If he wants issues clarified, they become clarified. Should he desire to encourage or motivate others, they feel encouraged or motivated following the interaction.

On the other hand, the incompetent person in this model is one who rather regularly and consistently finds that his impact on others is not what he has intended. He finds that for some reason he is fighting a series of unintended and unanticipated consequences. People are resistant, overly dependent, apathetic, hostile, fearful, frustrated, or cautious when he really would like them to be open, innovative, collaborative, and enthusiastic. Something is going on between the intention and the impact that requires some modification or adjustment.

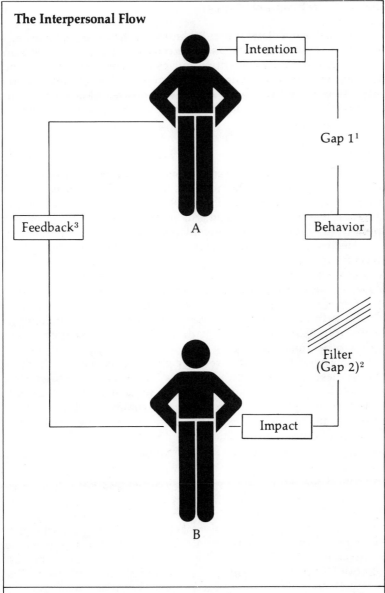

The Interpersonal Flow

1. Gap 1 is the difference between one's intentions and the behavior that represents them.
2. Gap 2 is the difference between one person's behavior and the other person's perception of it.
3. Feedback is finding out how our behavior has been received by others.

Interpersonal Style and Strategy

Almost immediately after an intention has been established, or developed in one's thinking as he perceives a situation, the behavioral implementation of that intention moves into operation. Occasionally a person will think through his strategy for achieving his intentions very carefully and will have a plan well devised. But more often he will move quickly into action, relying on his previous experience, intuition, or best guess.

Style

Style refers to the rather unconscious, habitual, consistent pattern of behavior that characterizes a person's performance. One person's style might be described as aggressively autocratic, another's as benevolently autocratic, and still another's may be rather passively introverted or reflectively contemplative.

Fiedler describes leadership style as "the underlying need-structure of the individual which motivates his behavior in various leadership situations. Leadership style thus refers to the consistency of goals or needs over different situations" (1967:36).

One's style is a rather constant feature of one's behavior and is usually such a part of one's actions that it is difficult to change. It is probably neither possible nor desirable to try to change a person with a rather quiet, easy-going style into a more aggressive, dominant person. The research data are clear on management and leadership effectiveness — people with wide variation in style have been and are successful in their positions. There is some indication that people with certain styles may have a greater chance of success in some situations than in others. A good match between one's style and the demands of the situation might be highly desirable.

Strategy

While his style may be rather consistent and difficult to change, a person's *strategy* or plan of action can be improved significantly. If one wishes (intends) an improvement of performance in others, one can plan a strategy of involvement — having people participate in the improvement program — or he can devise a threat strategy, such as threatening people with punishment or loss of reward if they don't improve. People with quite different styles can implement similar strategies. A quiet person can use threat as well as a loud, aggressive one. It is apparent that there is some connection between style and strategy, for a manager with an autocratic style may find it harder to engage in a participative strategy.

But people can learn different strategies of leadership behavior. Fiedler (1967) refers to leadership behavior in the same sense as we

4

talk about strategy. He says, "By leadership behavior we generally mean the particular acts in which a leader engages in the course of directing and coordinating the work of his group members. This may involve such acts as structuring the work relations, praising or criticizing group members, and showing consideration for their welfare and feelings."

A major obstacle to translating one's intention into an effective strategy and thus achieving the desired impact is the lack of clear feedback as to the actual result of the behavior. Subordinates often mask their real reactions to the behavior of the manager and pretend to support decisions or actions when in reality they are feeling negative and resistant. The more power, status, and influence a person gains, the more fearful subordinates and others are to share honest feedback about their reactions to actions taken. Methods for gathering feedback are discussed in a later chapter.

Unacted Intentions

It should be obvious that one cannot achieve desired impacts unless action is taken. There are people whose behaviors do not appropriately reflect their intentions because of their lack of skill, their inexperience, or their ignorance about useful strategies. There are also people who are afraid to take action and sit silently on their intentions wishing that something could be done, having fantasies of the great accomplishments that might be, but in the final analysis doing nothing. In a real sense inaction is a strategy — it is one way of coping with a situation, and it will certainly have an impact on others. It may not be the impact that one desires, however, and if one is going to be effective as a manager or change agent, he will need to plan a more appropriate strategy to achieve the desired impact in that particular situation.

How to Develop an Effective Strategy

It is not possible for anyone to be so all-wise, sensitive, and skillful that he will always know exactly the right things to do to produce the exact impacts or results he desires. However, it may be possible to develop a strategy that will help devise a further strategy to achieve the desired consequences. Following is an outline of how a manager or change agent might develop an effective interpersonal strategy in collaboration with those he wants to influence.

Declare Intentions

Instead of moving directly into the implementation of intentions, a different approach would be for the manager to bring together the people he is trying to influence to talk with them about what he would

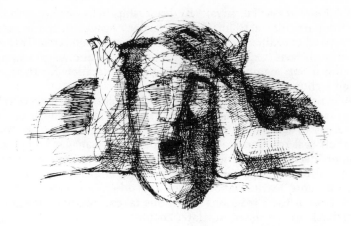

like to achieve. As a result of this discussion they would have a clear understanding of his intentions instead of trying to guess his intentions by interpreting his behavior. If subordinates have not experienced this new discussion of intentions before, their filter systems may cause them to look upon this action with suspicion — as another "gimmick" or trick. The leader must be completely candid in declaring his intentions clearly and then inviting the next step.

Make Suggestions for Action

The strategy to build a strategy next suggests that people be asked for their ideas, suggestions, and insights about how to achieve the desired results. If a manager's intentions are to motivate his subordinates to greater productivity, he might bring them together and honestly explore his intentions, what he desires, and why he desires it. He may find in that process that their view of the situation is quite different from his own. This discovery might cause him to revise his intentions. But, assuming the subordinates accept his intentions as valid, they would then offer their suggestions about what would be necessary or important in motivating them to increase their production.

Develop an Action Plan

From these suggestions comes a plan of action, the result of the collaborative action of boss and subordinates.

Argyris (1970) claims that the three characteristics of a healthy organization are these:

1. *The ability to gather relevant information.* A healthy organization has an open communication system that allows all data important to the achievement of effective action to surface and to be used in decision making.

2. *Free, informed decisions.* Healthy systems make good decisions based on solid data. If a system is not functioning well, people are afraid to raise all the legitimate questions or to disclose all necessary information about real conditions or attitudes, and as a result decisions are not sound. Also, if people feel pressured into making decisions with which they do not agree, the decisions are not based on free choice and the commitment to implement them is diminished.

3. *Commitment to implement decisions.* An organization may make good decisions, but unless there is commitment to follow through, together with a system of evaluation of results, even good decisions may not achieve the results intended. Sound organizations develop the capability to ensure the proper implementation of decisions to their appropriate conclusions.

If Argyris's analysis of the effective organization is correct, then a strategy which involves people in the design of strategy is more likely to result in better planning, sounder decisions, and greater commitment to carry out the action plans.

The competent person will stay in the relationship with others and work through problems of unclear intentions, inappropriate strategies, disruptive styles, or clogged filters. He will gather feedback on his impacts and devise better strategies to deal with undesirable consequences. Competency demands that a person work consistently to translate his intention into the desired impact.

References

Argyris, Chris
    1970   *Intervention Theory and Method.* Reading, Mass.: Addison Wesley.

Campbell, John P., et al.
    1970   *Managerial Behavior, Performance, and Effectiveness.* New York: McGraw-Hill.

Fiedler, Fred
    1967   *A Theory of Leadership Effectiveness.* New York: McGraw-Hill.

CONGRUENCE*

The term *congruence* is used to denote behavior that coincides with one's state of mind and feelings. Difficulties arise in achieving real congruence, which is much more than mere impulsive behavior like the reaction of anger to an unpleasant stimulus. Truly congruent behavior must be consistent with the whole range of one's value system, as well as one's feelings.

Being congruent does not mean that a person necessarily maintains his behavioral status quo. Rather, it demands that he express his dissatisfaction with his behavior to others and then try to change it. A certain skill is involved in the process of becoming congruent, and it is a skill which, like others, can be learned.

Social systems that do not support congruent behavior may need to be changed before people in the system can become congruent. In order to build greater trust in organizations, it is important for managers to develop greater congruence in their own behavior. Nothing undermines trust more rapidly or thoroughly than an awareness that someone is not what he pretends to be — that his behavior is not congruent with what he thinks and feels.

Congruent Behavior

The idea of congruence as defined by Rogers (1961) has generated a share of excited acceptance attended by some disturbing criti-

---

*Revised. Reprinted by special permission from *Journal of Applied Behavioral Science*. William G. Dyer, "Congruence and Control," 5(1969): 161–73.

cism. Rogers defines congruence as "the term we have used to indicate an accurate matching of experiencing and awareness. It may
still be further extended to cover a matching of experience, awareness, and communication. Perhaps the simplest example is an infant.
If he is experiencing hunger at the physiological and visceral level,
then his awareness appears to match his experience, and his communication is also congruent with his experience" (1961:308).

Rogers goes on to point out the disruption that occurs in a relationship where there is noncongruent behavior. If I think a person is
angry, yet he denies he is angry, my trust of him is diminished and I
become wary of him. On the other hand, if the person admits his
anger, which is consistent with my experience of him, then I feel he
is an honest, trustworthy person; my confidence increases; and the
relationship develops around feelings of trust and openness. Thus,
according to Rogers, congruence leads to the following general
principle:

> The greater the congruence of experience, awareness, and communica-
> tion on the part of one individual, the more the ensuing relationship will
> involve: a tendency toward more mutually accurate understanding of the
> communication; improved psychological adjustment and functioning in both
> parties; mutual satisfaction in the relationship (1961:311).
> Conversely, the greater the communicated incongruence of experience
> and awareness the more the ensuing relationship will involve: further com-
> munication with the same quality; disintegration of accurate understanding,
> less adequate psychological adjustment and functioning in both parties; and
> mutual dissatisfaction in the relationship (1961:313).

As I have presented this idea to many individuals and groups —
while indicating my own acceptance of the general idea of congruent
behavior — three main objections usually arise:

1. "Do you mean that a person should always behave exactly
as he feels? If I feel like punching you in the nose, raping your wife,
or yelling obscenities at you, should I go ahead?" The issue raised
here is this: *Does congruence mean giving in to all impulses immediately?*

2. "I have been taught all my life that I should learn to control
my anger or negative feelings. Suppose I don't like someone; if I
behave as though I do like him, then I will begin to like him. Suppose
I feel unhappy; if I try to act happy, after a while I will feel happier."
The issue here is this: *If I behave congruently all the time, will I ever
learn to improve on those behaviors in myself that I do not like?*

3. "That congruence bit sounds good, but it doesn't work. I
told my wife the other night that I was really upset with the sloppy
way I found the house every day when I came home from work. She
was so mad she didn't speak to me for three days, and I had to plead
for forgiveness and buy her a present and behave in all kinds of noncongruent ways before we got back on an even keel." The issue here

is this: *Congruence does not always seem to result in immediate improvement in relationships. Why not?*

Issue One: Does Congruence Mean License?

Central to the first issue is the question: Is congruence synonymous with license? Does it mean that it is all right for a person to behave in any way so long as it is consistent with his current state of awareness and experience? Congruence in this direct and immediate sense *has* become a major value for some. The hippies, for example, stress the hypocrisy of "society" and the lack of congruence they observe in conventional life. Behaving exactly as one feels — refusing to bathe, not working, taking drugs, freely exchanging sexual favors — is the usually represented symbol of the congruent behavior of the hippie subculture, although those acquainted with the movement contend it stands for much more than these stereotyped symbols.

Congruence as a value (implemented, it becomes a style of behavior), favored by Rogers, seems to stem from a set of other kinds of values that are represented in our culture as a counterreaction to certain common values. Eric Berne (1964) has popularized the superficial "games" that characterize many human interactions. The "games people play" are the opposite of congruent behavior, and it is just such phony behavior that has given rise to the notion of congruence as an antidote to the prevailing pattern.

We seem to be living in an emotionally deprived culture where the emphasis is on rational behavior to the restriction of emotional responses. Argyris (1962) and Gibb (1965), among others, have pointed out the dominance of rationality in the management of many organizations, with the resulting disruptive consequences as emotional behavior interferes with ongoing activities — because many persons prefer neither to recognize nor to deal with emotional behavior. Many of the writers who have pointed to this denial of emotional behavior in organizations have suggested that managers need to learn to recognize, accept, and deal more effectively with human emotions. In this sense they are suggesting more congruence — more openness of feelings and emotions, and a greater willingness to deal with these feeling-data openly and honestly. These arguments again are a reaction against those norms that support phoniness, maintenance of a facade, gamesmanship, and denial of feelings in behavior. But if congruency is a counter value, how far does it go? What are the limits, if any?

Congruency as a counter value is based on the fact of certain existing control orientations or value orientations already present in traditional society. While they are usually not explicitly mentioned, for most people there are certain already built-in control

features that result in congruency within limits. As mentioned above, the problem for many people is not going "too far" with congruency but dealing with overcontrolled behavior.

The great problem with issue number one stems from an assumption that congruency becomes if not the only value a person lives by at least the major value of import. At this level a searching examination of value systems for individuals and organizations becomes critical. One of the issues that has not been handled well is recognizing the personal value systems of participants. Congruency is suggested as a new value without really examining in any depth the other values people hold, including those values they perhaps should relinquish as no longer useful and those values they should cherish and retain.

When I am asked the question raised in issue one: "Do you mean that you are always going to behave exactly as you feel even if you feel like hitting someone or seducing someone?" I answer in this manner: "Being congruent is not the only value I hold. I also value the rights of others. My personal value system stands for trying to live a helpful life with others, to value a society based on mutual respect and acceptance. If I were to engage in behavior that might be

11

'congruent' at the moment, I would also violate a great many other values that I deem important. I will not violate those values just to be congruent."

The issue then becomes: How do I deal with my hostile, punishing, or devastating feelings? If I were to act them out directly, I would violate certain other values I hold as important. If I deny these feelings and try to repress them, I am aware that the result may be a number of harmful consequences either toward myself (certain psychosomatic difficulties) or in subtle, hostile reactions toward others that are difficult to handle since they are hidden or guarded and can easily be denied. Thus my definition of congruence would encourage me to *express my feelings without necessarily acting them out*. However, this behavior leads to the problem raised in issue two.

Issue Two: Does Congruence Allow for Change?

Here the issue concerns the matter of change. Congruence in its simplest form would require that each person behave according to his current level of awareness and experience. Sometimes we are not happy with that current level; we would like not to feel the ways we sometimes do. We would like to change our pattern of feeling, experiencing, and expressing.

From time to time I encounter a person who accepts certain things about himself as fixed — as a part of his "personality" that is almost immutable. He explains that he should not really be held responsible for the consequences of his actions since "this is the way I am."

This reminds me of the story of the scorpion who asked a frog to carry him across a stream.

"No," said the frog, "you'll sting me if I do."

"Of course not," replied the scorpion, "for if I do, you will sink and we will both be lost."

At that the frog agreed and began to ferry the scorpion across the water. In the middle of the stream the scorpion suddenly jabbed the frog with the fatal sting. With his last breath the frog asked, "Why did you do it?"

Replied the scorpion, "It's in my nature."

People are not scorpions (although some act the part), and we have learned that the nature of man is not fixed or unchangeable. A person who says, "I'm just a blunt person; if that hurts you, it's just the way I am," would seem to operate on the scorpion theory of personality. A congruence value would seem to give this type of person the perfect rationale to continue behaviors which are "just the way I am" regardless of their consequences to others.

When a person holds a complex of values, an experience will

12

often elicit a range of feelings. To what feeling should one be congruent? Suppose I have strong hostile feelings toward another person to the extent that I feel like punching him in the nose. At the same time another set of values elicits some feelings of guilt about the hostile feelings; these other values suggest to me that I should be trying to "love my neighbor as myself." In fact, these other values direct me toward a goal of trying to understand and accept others the way they are. I do not want to live my life responding in quick, hostile, punishing ways toward others, even if I currently feel that way. I do not want to adopt the scorpion theory that "this is just the way I am"; therefore I will be congruent, and this makes everything justifiable. Certain values suggest change. While congruency *seems* to have a nonchange orientation, congruency in a more complete sense, in my experience, becomes the real basis for change.

If I feel hostile and punishing toward another person and at the same time have feelings of concern or guilt for feeling this way in light of other values, congruency theory would require that I share *all* these feelings, not just the hostile ones. If I were truly congruent (and this demands that I be aware of *all* my own values and my range of feeling experience), I should express the range of feelings toward the person in words such as these: "John, when you try to dominate the meeting, I want to punch you in the nose. You make me feel very hostile and angry. But I don't like to feel that way. I also would like to accept you and work with you. How can I work out these feelings with you?"

Accepting and admitting that we do have certain "bad" feelings does not mean that we want to keep them or that we cannot change. My own experience tells me that expressing these feelings that I do not like and want to change, making them open to the person in question, results in a lessening of these feelings in me and allows me to respond more to the feelings I have that I like better. Should I go so far as to act as though I like a person, even though I do not like him, in the hope that this will result in liking? In light of the discussion above the answer would be no. I should share with the person both my feelings of dislike and my desire to like and engage in a continual interaction which will allow the liking feelings to be enhanced. This should be the result if there is any validity to the Homans proposition that liking increases with interaction (Homans, 1961).

There is also the matter of timing. Should I express all my feelings immediately? Does congruency demand immediacy of expression? A common experience for many is that if they "sleep on it" they will feel different later on. Some theories of personality would suggest that this lapse of time does not eliminate the feelings but allows the feelings to become buried in the unconscious part of ourselves. Others feel that through insight and self-dialogue we can resolve certain inner feelings without expressing them to others. This seems to me to be an interesting area for further research and analysis.

Can a person be congruent if he admits his feelings to himself but does not share them immediately and openly with the others involved? Can a person wrestle with his own feelings and the connected sets of values and win a private war within himself, or does congruency demand an open interaction? For me there is no clear answer to these questions. I think I have experienced both conditions. I think I have been able to silently examine my own conflicting feelings and achieve a sense of resolution or congruence, if you will, within myself. On the other hand, I have also experienced (usually in a laboratory setting) the exciting process of letting another person know immediately my feelings about his behavior with a resultant working through of the differences between us. In my experience this has led to a deepening of the relationship as described by Rogers (1961). It may be that the nonopen resolution of feelings toward another does not achieve an enhancement of the relationship, although it may result in a sense of resolution within.

One theory of emotional behavior contends that emotions if not expressed continue to persist and to expand if the "cause" of the emotion continues. I am referring to the commonly experienced phenomenon of a person who is continually irritated by another until he finally "can't stand it any longer." At that point there is an explosion of feeling that may actually be stronger than was originally warranted but was allowed to build up by the holding in of the feelings. If this is true of emotional behavior, then it would seem that resolutions of interpersonal conflict would result more easily if dealt with more immediately. It would also seem that if we would be more congruent in the earlier stage of the emotional experience, then our feelings at first would more accurately represent our reaction to the stimulus behavior. When expressed later on, the built-up emotion may not be a good representation of the feeling initially prompted by the behavior of the other. The "waiting game" may allow us to add fuel to the initial feelings as we begin via a selective perception process to see things in subsequent contacts. But then again, it may be that waiting for a time allows us to cool down and that the later emotion does more adequately represent a range of feelings and values if time is allowed for them to converge and interact within us. Again, more thinking and research seem to be needed.

Issue Three: Can Congruence Be Learned?

The hub of issue three seems to be: *How* are we congruent? Some people claim that they have tried congruent behavior and that the result has not been rewarding. Rogers (1961) feels that congruency will result in the enhancement of a relationship. It seems to me that there are differing ways or differing styles that people have of behaving congruently. Congruent behavior for Person A may appear to others as crude, blunt, and punishing, whereas Person B's behavior, also congruently oriented, may be perceived as open, helpful, and trustworthy. Is there not some element of skill in behavior? Is it possible in expressing our feelings toward others to learn ways that communicate better and result in reactions from others more in line with our intentions toward them? It appears to me that one of the reasons for a human relations laboratory is not only to help participants examine a new value like congruency and to see how it fits into their value structure but also to help them develop some behavior skill in implementing this new value.

In discussing feedback, Argyris (1962) points out what I have found to be an important factor in giving helpful feedback: namely, that we remain descriptive and nonevaluative. If this is true, we might then teach people to give nonevaluative feedback. This same condition may be true for all attempts at congruent behavior — that is, learning the skill of expressing our feelings in descriptive, nonevaluative terms. The process stemming from an interaction context may follow a formula expressed like this: "When you did this (describe the action), it made me feel this way (describe as accurately as possible the inner state you now experience)."

Many people worry about congruent behavior. "How can I present my feelings tactfully so I shall not hurt anyone?" "If I think through what I am going to say and choose my words carefully, then perhaps I shall not get into difficulty." This careful planning and choosing often results in a response that sounds guarded, cautious, rehearsed, and anything but authentic, congruent communication. The descriptive formula may be at least one method of allowing for more immediate, spontaneous congruency.

It should also be recognized that human interaction takes place in a social structure and that despite the skill of the one being congruent social norms and expectations may mediate against a positive response. Each of us interacts with others within the context of a social system where certain norms operate and where each person has a defined position or status and a role definition. The operation of the system expects certain consistent role performances. Some persons in subordinate role positions have reported going back home from a human relations laboratory and trying out new congruent behaviors with disconcerting results. The superiors continue to expect the old subservient behavior of a subordinate. These new congruent behaviors are totally unexpected and are perceived as threatening, and are thus responded to negatively. There is little system support for the new congruent behaviors, and in a short time the person reluctantly abandons the new congruency for the old, more rewarded role behaviors.

Goffman (1959), an astute observer of the interaction scene, describes the social order that exists when people perform as expected:

> Ordinarily the definitions of the situation projected by the several different participants are sufficiently attuned to one another so that open contradiction will not occur. I do not mean that there will be the kind of consensus that arises when each individual present candidly expresses what he really feels and honestly agrees with the expressed feelings of the others present. This kind of harmony is an optimistic idea and in any case not necessary for the smooth working of society. Rather, each participant is expected to suppress his immediate heartfelt feelings, conveying a view of the situation which he feels the others will be able to find at least temporarily acceptable. The maintenance of this surface of agreement, this veneer of consensus, is facilitated by each participant concealing his own wants behind statements which assert values to which everyone present feels obliged to give lip service. Further, there is usually a kind of division of definitional labor. Each participant is allowed to establish the tentative official ruling regarding matters which are vital to him, but not immediately important to others, e.g., the rationalizations and justifications by which he accounts for his past activity. In exchange for this courtesy he remains silent or non-committal on matters important to others but not immediately important to him. We have then a kind of interactional *modus vivendi*. Together the participants contribute to a single overall definition of the situation which involves not so much a real agreement as to what exists but rather a real agreement as to whose claims concerning what issues will be temporarily honored. Real agreement will also exist concerning the desirability of avoiding an open conflict of definitions of the situation. I will refer to this level of agreement as a "working consensus" (1959:9).

Goffman further claims there is a certain "morality" in behaving consistently with one's defined roles:

> In stressing the fact that the initial definition of the situation projected by an individual tends to provide a plan for the co-operative activity that follows — in stressing this action point of view — we must not overlook the crucial fact that any projected definition of the situation also has a distinctive moral character. It is this moral character of projections that will chiefly concern us in this report. Society is organized on the principle that any individual who possesses certain social characteristics has a moral right to expect that others will value and treat him in an appropriate way. Connected with this principle is a second, namely, that an individual who implicitly or explicitly signifies that he has certain social characteristics ought in fact to be what he claims he is. In consequence, when an individual projects a definition of the situation and thereby makes an implicit or explicit claim to be a person of a particular kind, he automatically exerts a moral demand upon the others, obliging them to value and treat him in the manner that persons of his kind have a right to expect. He also implicitly foregoes all claims to be things he does not appear to be and hence foregoes the treatment that would be appropriate for such individuals. The others find, then, that the individual has informed them as to what is and as to what they *ought* to see as the "is" (1959:11-13).

Here, then, is a real dilemma for the person who is suddenly confronted with a new value of congruency. This new value may be very appealing, and he may want to adopt it. However, those persons who surround him in his home, work, church, or community setting are not oriented toward this new value; they may expect him to perform as he has done in the past, and rewards will be contingent on a continuation of expected behaviors.

Thus the young husband who goes home and suddenly begins to behave congruently may be seriously violating a whole set of interaction expectations developed with his wife over a long period of time. It would be surprising if she began to respond positively from the first. What is necessary is the changing of the whole nature of the social system. The couple needs to develop together a whole new set of norms, roles, and expectations. The congruency theory would argue that the best way to begin this change is for the husband to begin the new behaviors and then work through the consequences with his wife. Other models of change would suggest that the change agent (the husband, in this case) should not impose change, but that change procedures be a collaborative effort agreed upon by both. It is not uncommon for a husband (or wife) who has attended a laboratory to try to get the spouse to attend also so that together they can begin a new pattern of behavior based on a common frame of reference. Many organizations use a laboratory experience for the same purpose: they send teams of managers to laboratories so that they can adopt new behaviors for the system based on a common new experience.

Summary

In this discussion I have been trying to look at some of the problems which a person who adopts a new value of congruency may expect to encounter. If these conditions are recognized, congruent behavior may be successful.

1. Congruency as a value is not the only value a person holds. To be congruent he must still behave consistently with old values or begin the process of reevaluation of his value system and begin to abandon or modify old values.

2. If one's values are in contradiction, the congruency stance is one effective method of beginning the process of personal value change. That is, one can begin to verbalize the ambivalence one feels and involve others in the process of examining the problems that result in the relationship.

3. Congruency does not mean that people cannot change. Certain values may support behaviors that we like better than others, even if we do not feel or behave in the desired way now. By expressing our current state of feelings and also our desires for improvement, we enter into a process that would seem to help us move toward the desired behavior goals.

4. Congruent behavior may take more skill than one now

possesses. One possibility is that learning to be congruent via a descriptive rather than an evaluative process may result in the type of response more consistent with the end result wished for in the relationship.

5. There are many conditions in the social systems within which interaction takes place which may be resistant to new, congruent behaviors. These structured role definitions and expectations may need to be altered through a change process before congruency as a reciprocal process can be engaged in by all.

References

Argyris, Chris
  1962   *Interpersonal Competence and Organizational Effectiveness.* Homewood, Ill.: Irwin-Dorsey Press.

Berne, Eric
  1964   *Games People Play.* New York: Grove Press.

Gibb, Jack R.
  1965   Fear and facade. In R. Farson, *Science and Human Affairs.* Palo Alto, Calif.: Science and Behavior Books, Inc.

Goffman, Erving
  1959   *The Presentation of Self in Everyday Life.* Garden City, New York: Doubleday.

Homans, George
  1961   *Social Behavior, Its Elementary Forms.* New York: Harcourt, Brace & World.

Rogers, Carl
  1961   *On Becoming a Person.* Boston: Houghton Mifflin.

FORMS OF
FEEDBACK *

Feedback is a process of data sharing in which a person receives *from others* information about his own behavioral performance. There are two parts to feedback: (1) the giving of data about the nature of the behavior, usually describing the behavior as a person sees or experiences it; and (2) the sharing of information with the person as to how the receiver felt about or responded to the behavior. The sharing of feedback data is not a new process, but a new term is being used. Recently the process has come under serious scrutiny to see what kinds of feedback lead to the most beneficial interpersonal results. Following are the types of feedback that we commonly experience.

Types of Feedback

Objective-Descriptive

Objective feedback is a process of trying to describe as clearly and objectively as possible the behaviors one has seen another person utilize. This is feedback in only the first part defined above; it does not tell a person the effect his behavior has had on others, but it is a reporting back to him that gives a description of his behavior as seen by an observer. Following are examples of this type of feedback:

---

*Revised. Reproduced by special permission from the July 1972 *Training and Development Journal*. Copyright 1972 by the American Society for Training and Development, Inc.

"You spoke only three times during the last hour."

"When you talk, you look only at the boss, never at anyone else."

"When you talk, you always look down or away but never directly at the person you are talking to."

"You tried to get into the conversation four times but never succeeded, and then you didn't try again."

This type of feedback attempts to give a person a mirror image of what his behavior is like. We are often not aware of the behaviors we utilize, and the purpose of this type of feedback generally is to help the person look more clearly at his own behavior.

A careful observer, through this feedback process, can help another person look at his behavior more carefully. An observer might tell a manager or group leader that at his last meeting Mr. Allen raised his hand three times but the leader ignored him. Or he might point out that the leader cut two people off, contradicted or rejected the contributions of three others, rephrased a proposition that had been made in his own language so it was different from the original, and then pressed for a vote when others said they wanted more discussion. Such a description might be very helpful to the person receiving the data, even though he did not get any information about how anyone actually felt about his performance. The receiver of the feedback is left to ponder the possible consequences or impacts of his behavior on others. The observer may report some consequential data, such as, "When you ignored Mr. Allen, I saw him pick up a paper and read it throughout the rest of the meeting; he never contributed again." The observer might also provide another type of feedback.

Assumed or Guessed

Assumed feedback shows the assumptions or guesses by a second-party observer as to what the impact of the person's behavior is. Some examples of this type of feedback would be the following:

"I think you hurt Mary's feelings. I saw her crying after you scolded her."

"I think that there is a lot of hostility and resentment toward you as a result of the way you conducted the meeting."

"If I were Joe, I would really be angry with you if you treated me the the way you did him."

The person receiving this type of feedback may find this helpful, for he may not have detected how people were feeling about his behavior. But it is also nonvalidated feedback; it is only a guess as to how people feel and think. A sensitive, insightful observer may be able to pick up feelings of others fairly well, but it is not the same as getting direct data from the object of the behavior. Although the direct feedback process allows the possibility of working through some differences not possible in the second-party guess, such guessed impact may give the person receiving the feedback some clues about what to do about his behavior in the future or may suggest some way to check out the actual impact on the person involved.

Second Party

From time to time a person may receive feedback about the impact of his behavior on others from someone other than the direct recipient of the behavior. It is a second-party report of data received from someone else. For example:

> "Tom told me that he was afraid to come into your office, for he always feels that you put him on the spot."
>
> "I talked with someone (I can't mention names) who told me that he felt very upset with the way you hog the limelight at staff meetings."

Second-party data has some built-in difficulties, even when it is perfectly accurate. First, there is always the possibility that it is not being reported exactly as the other person experienced it. Second, it is not possible to interact directly with the person to work through any difficulties. Such opportunities must be set up later. Third, the person reporting the data may be uneasy about the confidentiality problem. Although the person who had the experience may not have directly said not to report it, the second party doesn't know if he can legitimately tell who said it. Then the person receiving the feedback doesn't know if he can respond directly when the data he has received has come through a second party.

Direct Descriptive

Most people who have written about feedback have postulated that direct description may be the most useful form of feedback. It is a process first describing a person's behavior and then describing another's reactions to that behavior. It takes place directly between the persons involved. For example:

> "When you yelled at me just now, it made me feel very hostile and resentful toward you."
>
> "When you supported me on that motion, I felt very appreciative and good toward you."

The advantage of this form is that it gives the person receiving the feedback a clear picture of his behavior and what effect or impact that behavior had on the other person. It often opens up the opportunity to deal directly with the person and to have a chance to work out a resolution of any difficulty. Direct feedback must be accompanied by such conditions as a climate of trust and concern, a desire to improve the relationship, time to work on the issue, and comple-

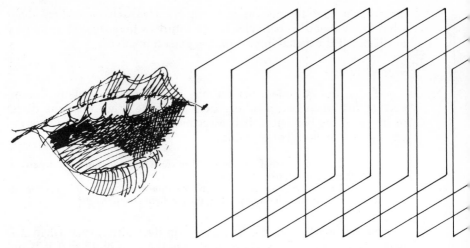

mentary expectations that such feedback is appropriate and desirable. The data is shared in a way that allows the person to work most easily with the information.

Sometimes we get feedback that is descriptive but represents only part of the total descriptive formula.

"I feel very uneasy with you."
"You make me feel inferior and stupid."

The person receiving such feedback knows how the other person feels about him, but he does not know exactly what kind of behavior produces the feelings. It is difficult to know what one can do to alter such feelings in others.

Direct Evaluative

When in the process of human interaction one person responds to the behavior of another, the response is often an evaluation or judgment one attaches to the behavior. Much feedback is in the form of a sharing of the evaluations or judgments one makes as a result of the behavior.

"You are really a rigid, authoritarian person."
"I think you are a cold fish."
"I think you're neat."
"I find you a very selfish person."

If feedback expresses one's feelings about another's behavior, descriptive feedback may result. If feedback evaluates the behavior, it represents one's judgments. When people first try to give feeling-descriptive feedback, it sometimes turns out like this, "Joe, when

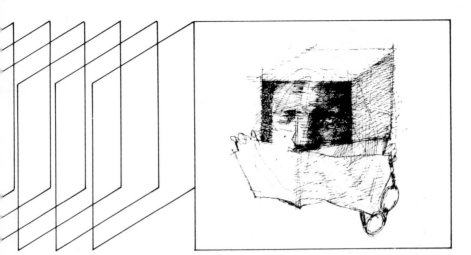

you push your ideas through at the meeting, I feel like you are a real dictator."

Even though the person uses the words "I feel like," he really is expressing his evaluation of the behavior. A person feels angry, hostile, jealous, uneasy, affectionate, tender. At least these are words we use to try to describe the emotional state inside us. We don't feel like someone is a dictator. This is a result of our thinking processes and represents a judgment of the behavior one has experienced.

Evaluative feedback may be very important data to receive, for it is sometimes difficult to know exactly why a person feels upset unless we know how he has evaluated the behavior. There is apparently a connection between our feelings and our evaluations, and knowing the evaluation is a key to understanding the feelings. If Bill thinks that people who initiate often, talk a great deal, and push for decisions are controlling, regulating, authoritarian types of people, he will resent such actions. Hal, experiencing the same behavior, will see such actions as helpful and facilitative. Thus a key to working out a relationship would be to understand Bill's evaluation of the behavior.

Direct Expressive

Feedback comes sometimes in the form of direct expressions of feeling about the total person.

> "I really like you."
> "I distrust you."

It seems that people sometimes respond to the total person and have generalized feelings about him. General statements are probably seldom if ever completely true. A person who says, "I like you," probably does not mean that he likes everything about the other person, just as a dislike reaction doesn't mean one dislikes everything about the other. However, these generalized feelings are important, for we probably experience and react quite differently to a person for whom we have a general feeling of liking than to a person we generally dislike.

If one is going to alter general negative feelings, it is probably important that he move the feedback into the more specific, descriptive area. He needs to know more concretely what he is doing that creates the negative reaction.

Nonverbal

Data are often returned to a person in the form of nonverbal cues he picks up from others. We see people smile, frown, turn away, fidget, turn pale or livid, or yawn as we interact with them. We see this as feedback about their reactions to us. Some people are sensitive to nonverbal cues, some insensitive, and others hypersensitive.

One must always be cautious in interpreting nonverbal feedback, for the meaning of the nonverbal reaction may vary from person to person, in fact from sender to receiver. When Bill nods his head, he may mean that he has heard the message, but Hal may interpret this as meaning agreement and support.

One person may frown and grimace when he is thoughtful or challenged by the ideas of another, but another person may see this as a sign of rejection. Since nonverbal cues are open to interpretation, they should probably be checked out with the sender, and feedback of a more specific type should be elicited.

Expressed in Performance

Nonverbal cues as described above are limited body cues that people give off in response to others. We can also receive certain performance cues that give us feedback about the effect of our behavior. The manager who finds that a subordinate is carrying out an assignment in a way quite the opposite from what the manager thought he said is getting feedback that his instructions were not clear or at least were not understood as he intended.

Again, these performance cues are initial feedback indications that things may not be going as we intended. We can learn from the performance cues that we may need to move the feedback process into a more intensive, descriptive level.

Expressed in Instrumented Data Collection

A feedback method that has long been employed by many organizations is the use of systematic data collection devices such as questionnaires, surveys, evaluation forms, and interviews. There are certain advantages and disadvantages to these methods. The tabulated responses give the person a picture of the reactions of many people to him. A manager may be able to see that ten of his fifteen subordinates feel that he spends almost no time in sharing information about changes that occur in the organization. It is also possible to gather some feeling data about a person's performance.

I have a strong personal reaction to John when —
1. He makes me feel angry or dominated.
2. He makes me feel involved and excited.
3. He makes me feel guilty or ashamed.
4. He makes me feel outmaneuvered or off-balance.

Many volumes have been written on methods of data collection, survey research, interviewing, scale construction, and others. It is not appropriate to review all those here. It is important, however, that when instrumented methods are used skill and care are practiced in developing valid and reliable procedures. Regardless of the accuracy of the collected data, there is always a limitation to this form of feedback as a means of improvement. The collected data are often cold and impersonal, and there is no real communication of the actual feelings involved. Data do not always connect the person *receiving* them with the person or persons *giving* them and do not allow the possibility of working through differences, which is always present in direct face-to-face sessions. Instrumented feedback is really just the beginning of the process of working on resolving differences between people.

Functions of Feedback

The above formulation describes various types of feedback that people often share with each other. A critical factor that influences the impact that the feedback has on another person is the motivation of the person giving the data. A person giving feedback to someone else should examine not only his method but his motivation. The form may be correct, but if the motivation is to punish or put down the other person, the impact may not be positive. Following are some of the major reasons why people give feedback to others.

To Punish, Hurt, or Put Down

When we are angry, hurt, or defensive, we may respond to the person or persons who have wounded us by giving feedback with the intent to get even or hurt or wound as we have been hurt. Evaluative feedback is probably most often used in such cases, but almost any type of feedback might be used.

> "You are nothing but a snob, and nobody I know likes you."
> "You make me sick; I just can't stand working with you."
> "I know that you have been trying to do a good job, but frankly you are just incompetent."

Feedback can also be given by changing the voice inflection and thus communicating a completely different message. Consider: "Thanks a lot; that was really a helpful suggestion." The effect of the statement could vary with the inflection — either to praise and support or to punish and put down. The person giving feedback should be aware of his own motivations and not pretend one motivation set when other feelings are really prompting his reaction.

To Reward and Support

Supportive or rewarding feedback is important not only in reinforcing behaviors we want to persist in others, but also in improving our relationships. Such feedback may be just a spontaneous expression of good feeling toward another person.

> "That was a great idea."
> "When you supported my position, I really felt good and I appreciated it."
> "I just want you to know that I like you and appreciate your work."

It would seem that such positive feedback would be most welcomed and that people would want to hear such reactions. However, there are people who find it very difficult to share such feedback with others, and there are also people who accept such feedback reluctantly and some who are always suspicious of the motives of people who give them supportive data.

To Help Another Improve His Performance

A common motivation stemming from current training programs is the sharing of feedback data out of a desire to help another person improve his effectiveness in his interactions with others. Out of this motivation, the feedback could be considered either positive or negative, but both are accepted because the person receiving the data feels that it is given in a spirit of helpfulness. One commonly hears a person in a training setting wanting to hear only the negative or critical feedback, for he has confidence that the people are trying to be helpful and he wants to know those behaviors that are creating problems for him.

To Improve One's Relationships

Feedback can also be a means of opening up some areas of difficulties between persons and beginning a process of improving the relationship.

> "I've been worried about our relationship. I've felt you have been avoiding me, and I would like to talk about it."
> "John, I've noticed you have been disagreeing with me almost constantly, and that really bothers me. What's going on between us?"

Consequences of Feedback

It should be recognized that just the giving of data in the form of feedback is no guarantee that conditions will improve. Feedback may result in the improvement of relations between individuals in appropriate change in behavior or perception (Dyer, 1969). However, if people are not skillful or if they do not stay in the situation and deal with the consequences of the feedback, interpersonal situations may worsen (Thibaut and Coules, 1952:770–77).

The ultimate consequence of feedback is to allow people to achieve greater effectiveness in interpersonal behavior. Some types of feedback seem to facilitate adjustment, harmony, and mutual acceptance more easily than others.

Different people may have developed a preference for one type of feedback or another. It may be important for them to see which forms they use and to consider which forms might be more useful. In particular, few managers regularly or consistently either gather or give appropriate feedback. It should also be mentioned that no good training program to help people examine their own style of feedback and practice better forms has yet been developed.

References

Anderson, John
1968   Giving and receiving feedback. *Personnel Administrator* 31:21–27.

Dyer, William G.
1969   Acceptance or change. *Human Relations Training News* 13.

Meyer, Herbert
1972   Feedback that spurs performance. In *The Failure of Success,* ed. A. Marrow. New York: AMACOM.

Thibaut, John W., and John Coules
1952   The role of communications in the reduction of interpersonal hostility. *Journal of Abnormal and Social Psychology* 47:770–77.

ELICITING FEEDBACK*

In one survey a group of managers was asked, "Would you like to know what you do that creates problems for the people with whom you work?" Over 90 percent indicated that they would appreciate such information. They were then asked, "Do you currently have a method, strategy, or procedure for finding out this information?" Less than 20 percent said that they currently have any method for determining their impact on others. This is a common dilemma. Most people would like information (feedback) about the impact of their behavior, but they do not know how to gather such sensitive data.

In much of our current organization life, people have learned to mask, hide, and cover up their feelings, particularly those toward people in positions of power and influence. Because of this, it is often difficult for a person to know what his true impact on others has been. He may see only the polite smile, the ready agreement, the apparent consensus and may assume, falsely, that the external feedback cues really represent the total impact.

The person with good interpersonal skills has ways of checking out the data to determine his actual impact and to ascertain whether the problem, if any, is in his own inability to communicate his conscious intentions correctly or if it is in the filter systems of others.

In the process of improving one's performance, probably no skill is more important than being able to gather accurate and honest feedback about one's impact on others. Yet this is also an area of

*Revised. Reprinted by special permission from the *Personnel Administrator*. William G. Dyer, "Encouraging Feedback," (June 1974).

sensitive skill, for most people feel fearful and inept when it comes to sharing their feelings about someone's performance with him directly.

It is not easy for a person in a lower-status position in an organization to go to a more powerful, higher-status person and give feedback that is unsolicited and presumably unwanted. The risks involved, from the lower-status person's perspective, are so great that unless the situation becomes intolerable or he is ready to quit, the safest course is to remain silent and hope the passing of time will improve conditions.

This silent strategy seems to be widely used for coping with people who have negative impacts on us. It is a minimal-change strategy that masks the real conditions and keeps frustration and negativism underground. And until they surface, the negative consequences of a poor relationship are difficult to deal with.

Techniques for Eliciting Feedback

If a person initiates a process where he asks for feedback and sets a climate where the other feels safe or even rewarded for sharing information, he is more likely to receive sensitive feedback. So how do you go about doing this?

Individual Direct Request

Probably the simplest method is to invite another person to a private, one-to-one session, which could be preceded by a written memo or verbal request stating the purpose of the meeting, thus giving the person time to prepare. (*Example*: Dear Ed, I would like very much to get your reactions to my management performance. Do you see anything I do that creates problems for others? Do you have any suggestions as to how I might improve my effectiveness? I'd like to get together with you next week to talk about it. I'll have my secretary call and set up a time when I can come to your office for a discussion. Thanks, Don.)

As this method is discussed with managers, they nearly all agree that they would appreciate their boss's coming to their offices for such a discussion. Others feel it would not be inappropriate to discuss the matter in the boss's office at a regular report or discussion meeting.

Written Request

A second method is to request (either verbally or by memo) the person to share his feeling in writing. (*Example*: "Ed, I'm trying to improve my own management effectiveness. Would you be willing to take some time out and write down any suggestions you have for my improvement? Try to be as honest as possible. I want the feedback and feel it's important to find out what my impact on others is, both positive and negative.")

In a direct request for either verbal or written feedback the person of whom the request is made may feel on the spot. If his boss is making the request, he may feel obligated to say something but be uneasy because of the risk involved. Direct request data are not anonymous, and the person may wonder how direct he can be without creating problems. To stimulate the feedback, the following technique can be used.

Priming the Pump

Priming the pump stimulates the flow of data by the sharing of data already known. This process was used in a training program where one participant was generating negative feelings in others. Every time a serious, deep, or sensitive discussion was under way, this man would sit with what was later described as a sneer on his face. It was apparent that the other participants resented it, and rumblings were evident.

The second day this man addressed the group. "Whenever I get emotional or nervous, I know that my face twitches. It's something I can't seem to control. Some people have said it looks like a sneer. Have you been aware of this?"

His comment provided a great releasing factor, and people talked freely about their reaction to him. It became easy for them to discuss his behavior since he had opened the subject and had some awareness of it. A manager could help release feedback in a similar fashion. (*Example*: "Ed, I have been told that I cut people off in staff meetings and appear to reject their contributions. Have you been aware of this? Have you seen anything else I do that disturbs people? Do you have any suggestions on how I might improve?")

Subgroup Meetings

To assure more anonymity, managers can divide the staff into subgroups of three or four people at a meeting. The subgroups meet for thirty to forty-five minutes following a request like this: "I am very much concerned about my effectiveness as a manager. I would appreciate it if you all could help me. At the next staff meeting I would like to have each of you get into a subgroup and identify my behaviors that seem to reduce the effectiveness of our operation. Would you also list those things that you like and would want me to continue?

"It would be helpful if you could give me any concrete suggestions for improvement. I won't be present while you meet, and you can just turn in a written summary to my secretary. No names need

be attached. I'm more interested in getting the information than in knowing who said it. If any subgroup would like to talk with me directly, I'd welcome that opportunity."

Total Group Meetings

It is possible for a manager to use his total staff at a staff meeting to discuss his managerial style and to give him suggestions for improvement. The discussion is usually a preplanned agenda item, and people are aware that it is going to take place. The dialogue is more open than in the subgroup format, and there can be more direct exchange between the manager and his subordinates. Such a meeting requires a general climate of openness, a spirit of dealing directly with human issues in an atmosphere of concern and mutual help.

The meeting's format can vary. The manager can summarize his impressions of his own style and ask for reactions. He can ask each person to express his reactions and share his feedback and suggestions. The group can form subgroups for a few minutes and then come back for a total staff discussion.

Instrumented Data Collection

The use of instruments provides another avenue for anonymous feedback. Here the manager or the personnel department circulates an instrument or questionnaire that gathers data about his managerial performance as experienced by peers or subordinates. Such instruments are the Blake-Mouton Grid, Likert's Four Systems, Hall's Telometrics Instruments, and the Dyer-Daniels-Moffitt Management Profile.

The data collected are tabulated and presented to the manager. Such information gives a general picture of impact but may not include any specific suggestions for improvement, nor will it provide specific information on how to improve rapport with any one individual.

The advantages of the instrumented process are that it can be given to a large number of people, it focuses on common problems, it can be repeated at a later date, and it protects the anonymity of the respondents.

Shared Assessment

In a technique similar to pump priming, the manager writes an assessment of his own performance and asks others to confirm or deny it, to share additional reactions, and to make any suggestions for improvement.

Sample memo: I have written up the following assessment of my performance as a manager. Would you please indicate whether you agree or disagree with the various points, what your own reactions are, and what suggestions you have for improvement.

As I see myself, I feel I do the following things well:

1. I am punctual and never miss appointments or keep people waiting.

2. I am dependable in taking care of assignments or requests given to me.

3. I am a hard-working person who has great dedication and loyalty to the company and its goals.

I also see the following critical things about my performance:

1. I am a rather closed person, and I don't communicate very much or very easily. I would like to improve this, but I'm not sure exactly how to do it.

2. I tend to cut people off in staff meetings and am somewhat

rejecting of new ideas. I'm not exactly sure how people see or react to this.

3. People are a little afraid of me and feel a bit uncomfortable talking with me. (I don't know what gives people that impression or what I can do to reduce it.)

Opposite each of these comments should be space for the reviewer's comments and suggestions.

Outside Consultant

Using an outside person is another common method for gathering feedback data. This person can be from outside the organization or from the company's training or personnel department but not usually from the manager's department.

The consultant can use a variety of methods to gather feedback. He can observe the manager in action at meetings, in problem-solving sessions, or in the work setting. He can interview peers and subordinates and get their direct expressions. He can administer instruments and tabulate a summary profile.

The advantage of the outsider is that he can often see things to which insiders have become oblivious and can probe in areas not accessible to the manager. A disadvantage is that the manager and subordinates may become dependent on the consultant and never learn to give and receive helpful feedback as a regular part of their ongoing relationship.

After Feedback

For most people, sharing data with a superior is an especially high-risk activity. When it is first attempted, the person usually watches his superior closely to gauge his reaction. And this reaction usually determines whether such feedback will be given again.

Listen, Don't Explain or Justify

There is a tendency to explain or justify actions when we receive feedback that we feel is unwarranted or stems from a misunderstood action. When you ask for feedback, the burden is on you to listen and try to understand. This does not mean you are obligated to believe or accept the information, but your responsibility is to try to understand why the other person feels and reacts the way he does. Defensive behavior usually stifles the flow of feedback communications, for it tells the other person you are more interested in justifying yourself than in understanding him.

Ask for More

Especially in the open, verbal feedback process, there is an opportunity to get additional information. If the person eliciting he data can honestly keep saying, "That's extremely helpful. Tell me more. Is there anything else I should know about that?" it will support and encourage the continual flow of feedback.

Express an Honest Reaction

The person giving the feedback often wants to know what your reaction is to the data he has presented. The best guideline is to express your honest reaction.

Express Appreciation and Plan for the Future

Acknowledge the risk that was involved for the person giving feedback and share your appreciation for his efforts. It is also a good time to plan ahead for future feedback sessions, which will probably be less disturbing and more productive than the initial encounter.

Sometimes the negative impact a person has is a result of an inability to translate his intentions into appropriate behavior. At other times the other person's misperceptions lead to undesired consequences. In either case the manager needs to discern the impact and engage in a process of exploring intentions, behavior, filter, and impact with the goal in mind of reducing negative effects.

Gathering feedback is the skill that starts in motion the improvement of impact. Several methods may be appropriate in stimulating a greater sharing of feedback from peers and subordinates. Such methods as personnel discussion, subgroups, written communication, instruments, and outside consultation assistance are available to the manager who is willing to take the risk to begin this sensitive, difficult, but much-needed process.

References

Anderson, John
  1968   Giving and receiving feedback. *Personnel Administration*. 31:21–27.

Dyer, William G.
  1972   Forms of interpersonal feedback. *Training and Development Journal*. 26 (July):8–12.

Meyer, Herbert H.
  1972   Feedback that spurs performance. In *The Failure of Success*, ed. A. Marrow. New York: AMCOM, 199–216.

ACCEPTANCE*

As has been discussed in the two preceding chapters, following the first wave of contact and interaction and the initial impact of people on one another comes one of the most common occurrences in a training group — the giving of feedback, or letting a person know the effect his behavior has had on others. It can almost be predicted that certain kinds of behavior will elicit first attempts at feedback: the silent or relatively nonverbal, the highly aggressive or structuring, the overtalkative, and the caustic or sarcastic.

Implicit in the feedback process is the notion of change — change in the person receiving the feedback. Feedback about one type of behavior goes something like this:

> Sam: "Joe, you haven't said anything much at all for the last two sessions. I get quite anxious when you don't say anything. Why don't you speak up more? I really listen whenever you do say something."
>
> Joe: "I speak up whenever I feel I have anything to contribute. I'm really a quiet person, and I just don't talk very much in groups this size."

Sam is giving appropriate feedback. He is telling Joe the effect his behavior has on others, and he does this in a descriptive, nonjudgmental way. Still there is a basic request for Joe to change. If Joe finds out that his quiet behavior makes others anxious, he must feel a certain pressure to change his performance and to increase the quantity of his verbal contributions. Joe could legitimately respond to

---

*Revised. Reprinted by special permission from *Human Relations Training News.* William G. Dyer, "Acceptance or change," 13 (1969).

the feedback this way:

> Joe: "If my quietness bothers you, why don't you change? Why can't you learn to accept quiet people like me? Why do I have to change to make you feel better?"

This presents the hub of a real dilemma on the interaction scene. If Joe's behavior "bothers" Sam (or a number of other persons), what should be the goal of the subsequent interaction?

1. Should Sam give feedback to Joe with the expectation that he should engage in some type of behavior change?

2. Should Sam assume that it is his own problem and try to expand his acceptance of Joe's behavior without giving him any feedback?

Within this dichotomy are a number of ramifications of the issue: Are there some types of behaviors that are so deeply a part of a person's "personality," so fixed and deep-rooted, that change is almost impossible? If such be the case, what are these kinds of behaviors? If we could identify them, it would seem that persons who encounter such unchangeable behaviors should concentrate on widening their margin of acceptance rather than expecting such persons to engage in behavior change. Exactly what types of behavior can be changed is difficult to assess. From my experience in groups, I recall a number of situations where certain behaviors posed a dilemma for the group.

> June was a quiet member. She said she was "just naturally" a quiet person and did not speak up much in a group setting. Other group members did not accept this, and she was constantly encouraged to try to change her behavior. It seemed that some group members took it as a challenge to get June to become more vocal.
>
> Alice was told that people experienced her as a rather cold and distant person. Group members felt they could not relate easily to her and were not drawn to her. She was contrasted to Mary, who was seen as a very warm, friendly person whom people liked and enjoyed. There was the direct implication that if Alice could be more like Mary she would be a more effective person.
>
> Tom was "blasted" in the first round of feedback for his constant attempts to get the group "organized." He had pushed hard to get the group to identify its goals, to set up some type of agenda of activities, and to start working and not just sit around discussing "whatever happens to come up." Tom said he was the kind of person who worked better when things were organized, but the group said he pushed too hard, and they resented his attempts to structure them.
>
> Kathy was told that she seemed to avoid any conflict in the group. She was seen as always trying to smooth over difficulties. It appeared that she agreed with people quickly and seemed to avoid any confrontation with anyone. Kathy claimed that she was the type of person who liked to get along with people. She said she did not like arguments and discord and would rather go along with something she did not agree with in order to avoid conflict.

All the above are real situations and have been replicated to a

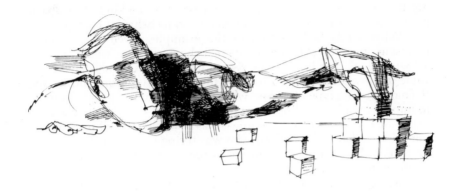

certain degree many times over in various groups I have observed. Which of the above types represent behaviors that can or ought to be changed?

A common stance taken in training is that we should be open with our feelings and give feedback about whatever our reactions happen to be. But what is the function of feedback? What is its purpose and how do we respond to it? If Sam gives Joe feedback about behavior that "bothers" Sam, what stance does Sam adopt while waiting for Joe to decide whether he wants to or can change? Does Sam just accept Joe the way he is whether he changes or not? If that is the case, why does Sam give Joe feedback at all — why not just accept Joe the way he already is?

And what about Joe? Having been given feedback about his behavior, what should he now do? He knows that Sam is bothered; if he doesn't change, how is Sam going to feel about him? Is he sitting back waiting for some sign of change?

Acceptance implies accepting a person the way he is, not the way we would like him to be. It could be argued that, if we accept a person the way he is and this is the essential condition for building trust and subsequently working together, then the basic process in human interaction is one of constantly expanding one's own margin of acceptance of others. Feedback, in the sense of implying change, would be superfluous. If feedback implying change is a basic interaction process, then what is it about the other person we accept? If we accept this and not that, what determines the value of the one over the other?

Here we face an important matter of values. What we do or do not accept in the behavior of others depends, in part, on what we value, what we consider appropriate, right, acceptable. If a person engages in behaviors that we find nonacceptable, it would seem that we should begin to examine our value system to see whether it is possible to alter the values upon which our reaction is based. If that is not possible, we may then need to engage in some kind of feedback process which leads to the working out of some behavior change.

What kinds of behaviors in the examples given above would represent unacceptable behaviors — behaviors that would violate a basic value? For myself, the two situations that would have some value implications for me would be those involving Tom and Kathy. If Tom were the type of person who wanted to control people, wanted to impose his ideas and opinions on others, this would violate a basic value for me. Tom might see himself as just being "well organized," but if I experienced him as one who was trying to control my thinking or actions, I would need to engage in some direct feedback and work on the issue between us.

Kathy may see herself as just a pleasant person who likes to get along with people, but if I experienced her as a person who held her feelings inside and did not share them and pretended to behave in ways inconsistent with her feelings, this would violate a value for me and would lead to my initiating feedback to her.

For behavior that I initially experience as "bothersome," I should try to examine my own values and see whether I need to try to expand my margin of acceptance or whether the behavior hits at an area important enough to be mentioned in the process of feedback. At that point I should be the one to initiate the feedback. In a training setting I have often responded to a request for feedback and have shared negative feelings even when they did not violate a value. When the other person initiates a request for feedback, I feel that he has a right to find out how his behavior affects others, and my values would lead me to share the data I have about him. If he asks me how I experience him, I should want to give him the feedback data and also tell him whether the behavior just "bothers" me or whether I experience it as a violation of certain basic values for me.

Feedback, then, is not just a request for change in behavior but the beginning of a process of acceptance or change, if needed. I have often seen a group give a person a great deal of feedback and a few days later comment to him how much change they had experienced in him. Probably an outside observer would have detected very little actual behavior change. Interestingly enough, following the feedback session the previous "bothersome" behavior was no longer such a source of irritation, even though the person had probably not changed much. This suggests to me that one of the critical functions of feedback is as the beginning of the process of acceptance. It seems that we can accept behavior much more readily if we can talk about it openly and if the person receiving the feedback accepts it — that is, if he is willing to hear it and take it into account. This seems to be the start of accepting behavior between the persons involved. I am thus defining feedback as not just a process of requesting a person to change but the beginning of a process of wider acceptance of others.

References

Pryor, Margaret, and Bernard Bass
    1959   Some effects of feedback on behavior in groups. *Sociometry* 22, no. 1:56–63.

Zajonc, Robert
    1962   Effects of feedback and probability of group success on individual and group performance. *Human Relations* 15, no. 2:149–61.

INTERDEPENDENCE *

Somewhere between the chaos of anarchy and the tyranny that insists on total dependence lies the realm of interdependence (the important balance between persons in authority and subordinates). Interdependent people acknowledge both their own strengths and shortcomings and those of others, and all are willing to do what they can to achieve common goals. It is an area of activity much to be desired, for it allows everyone to participate, to feel important because he is important, and to accomplish the purposes of an organization.

Consider the following example of a new employee:

> Tom is new on the job. He feels he is intelligent and capable and that with time and experience he will be a good salesman. But at the same time he is scared — he doesn't want to make any dumb mistakes. Running through his mind are two contradictory questions about his course of action: "Shall I go and tell the sales manager that I feel I really need someone to help me? Or shall I just strike out on my own and prove to everyone that I can do as good a job as anyone else? Will others interpret my asking for help as a sign of weakness? If I do ask for help, will they let me handle things my own way later on?" Tom sits, pondering, deep in his dilemma.

Conflicting Needs

These two crosscurrents are present in all of us — the need to be free, independent, and capable of doing things on our own; and the need to be dependent, to have the right and the luxury of putting our-

---

*Revised. Reprinted by special permission from the *Ensign.* William G. Dyer, "Interdependence: A family and church goal" (February 1971): 35–39.

selves into the hands of others when our own resources are insufficient.

A manager, seeing these apparently conflicting needs in others and depending on his understanding of himself and the people he leads, will respond in ways that may or may not result in the growth of a particular subordinate. It is *from* the authority person that the subordinate person is trying to break free to demonstrate his own competence, and it is *to* the authority person he must go when he needs support and assistance. Central to the performance of any leader — supervisor or executive — is the manner and method he uses to respond to the needs of others.

Dependence

Some managers' styles of behavior reinforce and support the dependency of their subordinates, with the long-range consequence that the subordinate remains incapable of functioning adequately on his own. For example, Sam Wilson drops into his boss's office almost every day, just to "talk things over" and get an opinion on the work he is doing. These regular visits have been going on for some years and are very satisfying to Sam. He feels his boss likes to be consulted and asked for advice, and he has found the daily consultation has kept him from making some pretty serious mistakes.

This example points out some of the elements of a strong dependency-development relationship. The person in the authority position (in this case the boss) may be using the subordinate person to meet many of his own needs. He would probably be indignant and hurt if it were suggested that he was selfish, for being selfish in the sense that he is concerned about himself at someone else's expense is not part of his conscious motivation. But in a real sense he may be selfish, for unknowingly he has been meeting his own needs without considering the long-range well-being of his subordinate.

There are times when dependency is legitimate and useful. Occasions will arise in which a person needs help beyond his own resources. All of us must at times depend on others — doctors, teachers, counselors, repairmen, friends, parents — when conditions face us that are beyond our resources to handle effectively alone. Dependency becomes crippling when a person no longer seeks to develop his own resources and to move to a more collaborative stance with persons in authority but automatically assumes he cannot do anything without the guidance, support, and influence of others.

All human beings start out in life from a position of almost complete dependency on others. The development of the child away from complete dependency is the responsibility of the adults who occupy positions of authority over him. *How to use authority to help others grow is the major challenge of every person in a position of authority.*

Too often authority persons become concerned with the wrong

goals — parents want children who are only well behaved; teachers want only quiet classrooms or students who will do and say what the teachers want; administrators want subordinates who will obey without question, who are yes-men. One way to achieve these goals is to create dependency in others. Interestingly enough, many dependency-producing leaders never recognize their part in the problem, for they will often exclaim sadly, "What we need is more people who will take initiative and won't just sit around waiting to be told what to do."

Counterdependence

In the other behavioral stream is the desire to be free, to "let me do it by myself." Some have postulated, as did the English philosopher Thomas Hobbes, that by his very nature a man is at war with everyone else as each tries to hammer out his own ego-centered world. If everyone actually were to do only what he wanted, without taking others into account, the result would be anarchy.

As managers see in their subordinates the tendency to seek freedom, they often try to stifle, reduce, or change it. There seems to be a subtle (and sometimes not so subtle) struggle going on between the leaders, who want to channel or control, and the subordinates, who want to be independent and free to do as they please. It is this basic struggle that underlies counterdependency. Some people get caught up in a resistance pattern to each authority person and expend much time and energy finding ways to resist him. They can always find a reason why the desires of the authority person can't or shouldn't be carried out, and they act accordingly.

Sometimes a negative response is the result of a wrong approach by the authority person. Perhaps he initiates directions to the subordinate in a way that is demeaning and robs him of personal dignity. Often no allowance is made for questions, discussion, or dialogue; the boss wants his worker to obey "with no back talk." Such an attitude creates in many persons a strong rebellious reaction.

A leader may deliberately create situations where the subordinate questions or resists, so that the leader can "show who is boss," thus gaining a kind of secret delight in dominating another human being.

It should not be assumed, however, that resistance and reaction are always the fault of the authority person. Often he may be behaving in a very appropriate manner, but the subordinate, conditioned to resent and rebel against authority, always responds negatively. Sometimes, in order to achieve a new and more effective level of interaction, both subordinate and authority persons need to reexamine their attitudes and behavior and work out a change.

How to Develop Interdependence

An ideal relationship that is both possible and desirable between authority and subordinates is called *interdependence* — the cooperative or collaborative use of each other's resources. Independence is not an appropriate term, for it suggests that the subordinate is freed from those in authority and goes his own way. Independence is not the most effective action in today's world — whether it be in family, school, church, business or government organization, community, nation, or world. Of necessity we are an interdependent people. Unfortunately, most people have not learned to be interdependent with others. Writers and researchers in the field of human behavior suggest the following actions to be taken by people in authority who wish to encourage greater interdependence.

Care and Concern

Any subordinate person must know that the person in authority over him really cares about him, not just about whether he does what he is told.

Concern for the individual should be unconditional although we may not care for certain of his actions. Too many authorities present conditional concern as the basis of a relationship: "I will accept you only on condition that you do what I want, will be dependent on me, and will meet my needs." Such a basis results in either dependency or rebellion.

Trust

Authority persons need to have greater confidence and trust in those under them. Leaders should trust their subordinates to make correct decisions and should give them the opportunity to do so. The authority who lacks trust, fearful that others will make mistakes or won't do the job the way he would, hovers around, watching and checking up, and makes everyone feel self-conscious and resentful.

Trust means allowing — allowing others to perform with a sense of confidence that they are supported by the person over them. Trust means being consistent and trustworthy so the person being directed has confidence in the words and actions of the authority person.

Open Communication

A vital ingredient in interdependence is the open sharing of information. Communication implies a sender and a listener, with understanding between the two. When interdependence is working, both authorities and subordinates have a chance to send and to listen. It is not a one-way communication system where the authority tells and others are always supposed to listen. We need to share our thinking and our feelings. On almost every subject or issue people have thoughts, ideas, or opinions as well as feelings. If we want true understanding, we must share both kinds of data.

Many leaders share few of their own feelings or ideas with others. Giving directions, orders, and commands is *not* sharing. Sharing comes first, before decisions are finally made. It is the process of getting thoughts and feelings out in the open so a good decision can be made.

Before anything is decided, the authority person should say, "I want to know what you think and how you feel about the issue at hand. I truly want this information. I will not judge you or punish you for being entirely truthful and candid. If we can all put our cards on the table, and if we really have concern for one another and trust one another, we can come up with solutions that will be satisfying to all."

Shared Decisions

Interdependence requires that decisions be made in a collaborative way, with all participants understanding each other and coming

44

to a solution they feel good about and are willing to support. Shared decisions are not necessarily fifty-fifty decisions, in the sense that each person will always demand an equal part in everything. Sometimes the manager will say to a subordinate, "You have more experience with this problem than I do; I trust you to make the decision and I'll support it." At other times the subordinate will respond similarly to the boss, and at yet other times each will have to listen to the other and work out a solution both can support and implement.

Joint Action

Interdependence means working together, which is necessary for the carrying out of decisions. In too many organizations leaders *tell* their workers what to do. The leaders pressure, control, or punish until their subordinates do what they demand. Too little work is planned and carried out together, so that all may experience the delight of a team effort, the accomplishment of things done collaboratively. Sometimes the work requires effort alone, but it is more satisfying if it can be shared with others.

We see all around us the consequences of people in rebellion. Either they are in revolt against authority, or they have never learned to work with authority persons. Training in collaborative problem solving and team effort should be taught in the home but can be learned on the job. It does not mean that leaders allow others license to do whatever they please, nor does it mean that subordinates slavishly carry out the whims of their leaders. Rather, it is a solid condition of mutual effort based on concern and trust.

References

Bennis, Warren G., et al.
  1964   *Interpersonal Dynamics.* Homewood, Ill.: Dorsey Press.

Gibb, Jack R.
  1965   Fear and facade: Defensive management. In R. F. Farson, *Science and Human Affairs.* Palo Alto: Science and Behavior Books.

MOTIVATION

People often face motivational issues no matter what their professions and interests. This chapter explores some ways to motivate others.

Desired Types of Change

The basic issue in motivation is a fairly simple one. In familiar terms, the question is "How can Ted influence (motivate) Herb to alter his performance?" How do the Teds go about getting the Herbs to change in (a) the quantity of performance, (b) the quality of performance, or (c) the direction of performance?

Quantity of Performance

A common remark I hear from mothers is "How can I get my children to do their homework, clean up their rooms, help in the house, and do the other things around here I want them to do?" Or I hear from teachers, "How can I get my students to get their work done, to write their papers, and to do more than they are doing now?" The same is true of industry and business. "How can we motivate an employee to increase the quantity of his performance?"

Quality of Performance

Sometimes the use of motivation is not so much "Can we get them to do more?" but "Can we get them to do it better?" "My subordinates do such a sloppy job. They get a certain amount of work done, but the quality is not good." "My children clean up their rooms, but the result is almost worse than when they started. How can we get them to do better?" So, at times, we are concerned about the quality of performance.

Direction of Performance

There are times when we are concerned about a change in the direction of performance: "I wish I could get my son to spend more time on schoolwork and less time on basketball." "I wish I could get my daughter to be more interested in homemaking skills and less interested in boys." Because we have a concern in changing the direction of performance, we turn our attention to motivation. How can we motivate people to shift direction from one focus to another, or how can we get people to improve the amount or quality of what is done? We are concerned about what we can do that will make some difference in the performance of other people.

Direct-Influence Processes

One possibility in dealing with motivation is that we try *direct influence*. We take some kind of direct action with the person or persons in whom we are trying to generate some change. Kelman (1961:57–78) has identified three major kinds of influence processes that many of us tend to employ. He uses the terms *compliance, identification,* and *internalization*.

Compliance

The compliance process is one of reward or punishment. You try to get people to comply with your request by promising rewards or threatening punishment. If they do comply, you increase reward and decrease punishment. This is a common influence strategy: "If you kids don't shape up and get your work done now, there is no TV for the next three days." "Unless production improves, there will be no bonus this year."

In our house, when our children were younger, my wife and I would have liked for our children to get up in the mornings, get dressed, clean up their rooms, finish their schoolwork, help get breakfast, help clean up the dishes, and go off to school happy and joyful. It somehow just didn't seem to work, and so we had a strategy that went something like this: my wife would say, "All right, kids, come on, get breakfast." Nothing happened so she would send me downstairs. We operate from a kind of decibel theory of motivation; that is, when the voice reaches a certain pitch, "All right, move!" they really start moving.

Our children have us well trained. They know that if anything is really important we, the parents, will respond. It is like the car-

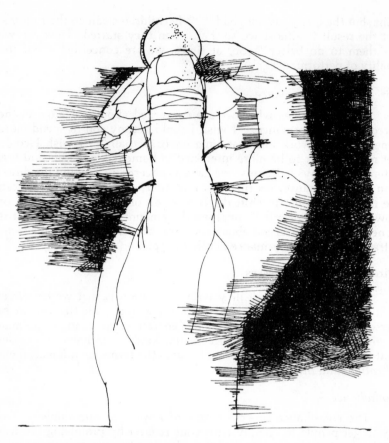

toon of two little brothers in their pajamas up in the bedroom playing, and one little brother says, "If Daddy doesn't get up here and make us get dressed, we're going to be late for school." When we start to yell, implicit in this is "We had better move or they'll get mad, and that isn't very pleasant," so they move. This is the compliance process.

In schools we often make this process fairly uniform and regiment it in terms of grades. Students come in, and we tell them what they have to do if they want to get an *A*. Then we tell them what can happen if they don't get their work in. This system is a fairly straightforward distribution of rewards and/or punishment. By the time students get to college, they are pretty well conditioned to the process and so they comply. Motivation to them and the teacher means compliance. They are motivated to get the reward. When they move into the world of work, they take this attitude with them.

The problem with the compliance process is that we often want people to do things for reasons other than receiving a reward. We want them to learn something because we think the material is important, not just to get a good grade. If we have available to us certain rewards and punishments, we can then make them available or withhold them in some kind of exchange. People know this and are "motivated" to change their behavior in the directions of whatever we'd like in order to get the reward or to minimize punishment, but not out of real commitment.

Identification

In the process of identification the basis of influence is in the nature of the relationship. The classic statement of identification is found in the New Testament, where Jesus says, "If you love me, keep my commandments" (John 14:15). This is a classic "identification statement." All of us have known or have had the experience of thinking, "George is such a wonderful person that I would do anything he would ask me to do, even if it were stupid, because I think so much of him." Or, "Mr. Johnson has always been so good and so considerate that I would be willing to do anything for him." Sometimes we find ourselves using this in a somewhat blatant kind of way. We may say something like this: "Now, I'm your mother; if you really love me, you'll remember all the good things I've done for you, and you'll do this for me." We may remember this in our own experience with our mothers and fathers. If we didn't do what they wanted us to do, it would interfere somewhat with our relationship. Now, identification overlaps into the compliance area because it can be a form of reward or punishment. The sense of identification with a person is the willingness to be influenced because of our faith and confidence in the other person and not because of the reward or punishment. If we are going to use the process of identification, we have to be sure we have the basis of a relationship at our command; otherwise our influence won't accomplish much.

Internalization

Internalization is based on the legitimacy of the argument. We are influenced by another person because the request he makes of us agrees with our own values and beliefs, and not because we are worried about rewards and punishment.

One Sunday morning I came up to get my family ready for Sunday School, and my wife said, "You'll have to talk to David." (David was seven years old at the time.)

I asked, "What's the matter, David?"

He said, "I'm not going to Sunday School."

"Why don't you want to go to Sunday School, David?"

He said, "I hate Jeff." (Jeff is our next boy who is three years older. They had had some kind of fight and he hated Jeff, so he wasn't going to Sunday School.)

I wanted to see what condition would motivate David to go to Sunday School, so I said, "Come on, David, I want to talk to you." We went out on the porch and I said, "David, would you go to Sunday School if I said, 'If you don't go, I am really going to paddle your pants hard'? Or would you go to Sunday School if I gave you a dime? Or would you go to Sunday School if I said, 'Look, as your father, it would make me feel good and I'd appreciate it if you would go'? Would you go if it would make me feel better? Would you go to Sunday School because you really feel that is where you ought to be on Sunday, that it is the right place to learn the things you need to know, and that down deep you really know that Sunday School is the right place to be? What would get you to go to Sunday School?"

David held up ten fingers.

I said, "The dime, huh?"

"Yeh," said David.

So I said, "All right, if you go to Sunday School, I'll give you a dime." But that bothered me, because he was responding out of compliance. Motivation that comes from compliance may be a violation of our own values.

Years ago, when I was an undergraduate student, I heard, "There is no greater treason than to do the right thing for the wrong reasons." This is how I feel about people being motivated for certain kinds of reasons. To have my boy continue to go to Sunday School for a dime would be a kind of treason. I'm not sure that what I wanted to achieve out of this situation was just to be able to get him in Sunday School.

There is another element in motivation: "What is it you are attempting to accomplish in motivation?" Are you just trying to get conforming performance? If you are, then you may want to continue to use compliance. But you may never be sure that what you really want to achieve at a deeper level is going to get done. You may find that people comply just to get a reward. The issues and the research are not clear about this. Allport (1937) developed a notion called *functional autonomy*: that is, some things we do under initial motivation later become autonomous in and of themselves. If we can get a boy to go to Sunday School for a dime over a period of time, after a while he may enjoy going to Sunday School; it will become a rewarding experience in itself. Possibly we use compliance initially as a means of building enough experience so the individual is eventually motivated by deeper values. That is what we hope, but we need to be very careful in using this strategy. If we are not careful, we often move into a bargaining situation — it will cost us fifteen cents the next time, then twenty cents, then a quarter. We move backwards rather than getting him more and more involved in the desired experience.

I was talking with an administrator for a volunteer organization, and he told me that different chapters come from many areas for central meetings. When they take a standing attendance (have people stand up from each of the chapters, count them, and give recognition to the chapter that has the greatest attendance), attendance is 30 percent higher than when they do not take a standing roll call. Now, if you are a practical administrator, what is your reaction? On the one hand, you might say, "It is a lousy kind of motivation that influences people to come to a meeting just to get their chapter's attendance counted." But on the other hand, you might argue, "Isn't it better to get 30 percent more in attendance by using a compliance device than not having them there at all?" This is a management problem with which almost everyone is confronted at some time or another.

What method of motivation are we going to use and what does it do to our own values as we try to influence people? I see my wife and me, eager to get some help from the children, resorting to all kinds of devices. We would like to have the children help in the home because they want to keep the house lovely, but at times we find ourselves reverting to motivational strategies that are not first on our list. What I sometimes find is that we start with compliance and move to other strategies. Before people really build much of a relationship, the initial motivation process is often direct compliance. It may be that we go through steps in motivation, going from the least desirable to the most desirable. However, I have never been able to demonstrate the sequence. I do have a feeling that we should somehow move to a higher level. I think it would be more consistent with my own values. Ultimately, it would be a more consistent system of motivation with my values to get people to respond because of the legitimacy of the argument. I think that sometimes we don't really allow this to emerge. We keep maintaining motivation at a fairly simple compliance level, the threats and reward become much more subtle, and there is a form of internalization. But the compliance is still there.

I listen to graduate students who say, "Let us work out our own design for our master's program; we are mature adults." But underneath this is "You'd better get going and do things the way the professors want, because if you don't they can wash you up in this school. You'd better be very careful."

Sometimes we think that people are operating on a higher level, but we have overlaid a heavy compliance process that is really moving them along. If we want to finally move to this different kind of motivation, we have to work on the internalization process. We have to deal with it directly and allow people the chance to operate from what they really think and believe. This is often awfully hard for people who are in authority positions to do.

Similarly, it is sometimes very difficult for my wife and me to allow our children the right to make their own decisions. Hopefully, we have moved them to a point where we can react as we did to our children the other night. We have three teenagers that date, and one of the boys said, "What time do you think we ought to come in after our dates?"

I said, "I think that you ought to be in about 1:00."

They replied, "If we're double-dating, and the dance doesn't get out until 12:00, and we're driving the car, how do we get home by 1:00?"

So I said, "All right, I trust you. I think you are mature enough to decide when you should be home."

Am I really saying, "You have the right to make your decision as to when you come in"? But underlying this is, "Boy, if I get up and it is late and you are not in, you and I really are going to tangle!" This is an interesting issue to look at. If we are trying to influence people to motivate themselves on the basis of the *legitimacy of the argument*, to what extent do we still have a "loaded pistol" at their heads? The pistol constitutes direct compliance influence.

The Process of Altering the Situation

A second kind of influence process is trying to motivate people not by pushing directly at them, but by altering the situation. This is an extremely interesting strategy for a person who is trying to get another person to improve or alter his performance. Let me describe some possibilities here. In one research project, the researcher was working with a branch bank and wanted to see if he could get the employees who put out the monthly bank statements to improve their performance. On the average, these people worked from 8:30 to 3:30 every day and were getting out 100 bank statements a day. Management was concerned with improving the *quantity* of performance. The practical question was, how could the employees be motivated to produce more bank statements? What are some possible strategies?

1. If they get over 100 done, pay them extra money — compliance — but the bank officials didn't want to do that.

2. Isolate them so that they couldn't waste their time. This would be altering the situation. The officials didn't want to do that either.

3. Finally they followed this procedure: Company officials told the employees, "As soon as you get 150 bank statements done, you can go home." On the average, they were able to finish and go home at 1:00 p.m. Time was a much more important factor to them than other rewards, but to change this factor also meant altering the nature of the workday. The required minimum of workday hours had to be redefined.

Sometimes we don't pick up ways of altering the situation. We get so involved in attempts at direct influence through what we say, or how we can push, that we don't think of restructuring the situation.

The bank officials looked at the quality of the employees' work and found no drop-off even with the increased output. The quality was every bit as good as it had been before. What they failed to anticipate, incidentally, was that letting some people go home at 1:00 affected the other people in the system who did not go home early. It is like letting one child stay up and watch television and making the other stay in the bedroom and do his work. There are repercussions in the system. One part of the system has one type of motivation condition and another has a different condition; the disparity can lead to disruptions in the system.

Let us look at another motivation theory, that of Frederick Herzberg (1966), who says that in any organizational situation there are two sets of factors: one creates satisfaction or dissatisfaction, and one creates motivation. The person trying to improve motivation often starts by working on the satisfiers in the situation and neglects the motivation factors.

Herzberg asked people what made them unhappy or dissatisfied in their work. They gave such answers as "We don't have a good relationship with our boss, we don't like the people we are working with, the work is dirty, we don't like our salary." If the situation is improved and people are given good working conditions, good supervision, good salaries, and pleasant working relationships, feelings of satisfaction result. Herzberg claims making people satisfied does not motivate them. They feel better about the working conditions, but they don't work harder, they don't work with better quality, and they don't change directions.

A major problem in organizations is presented by people who manage — parents, teachers, or administrators — when they try to alter the situation by manipulating the satisfiers. Herzberg says that what motivates people is to be given a job that is challenging, rewarding, and leads to advancement and growth. Motivation lies in the nature of the work they have to do. If we assign people meaningless, routine, mundane work and we want them to do more of it, it is hard to provide motivation. Herzberg makes a strong case for what he calls *job enrichment*. Many organizations are attempting to enrich the job so that people are motivated because the work itself is more challenging and rewarding.

Some things Herzberg has done with organizations have been interesting. Instead of having workers do just one kind of task, he gives a group of workers the responsibility for an entire activity. They have to organize, plan, distribute, and so forth. Their motivation increases because they now have something that is challenging. Sometimes our strategy when something isn't done very well is to break down this meaningless something into even smaller bits so it will be easier. But this doesn't motivate. The issue Herzberg raises is that, if we can increase the complexity, the challenge, the responsibility, and the recognition that a person gets in doing something, only then do we deal with motivation. If we are going to alter the situation for people, we should think about enriching it.

Motivation through Higher Needs

Maslow (1943:370–96) says that all of us have basic needs: physiological, safety, social, ego, and what he calls self-actualization. These needs are in a hierarchy from lower needs — physiological — to the highest and most complex — self-actualization. Argyris (1957) says that what happens in most organizations is that conditions are established that are geared to satisfy the lower-level needs, and people's higher needs go begging.

Some people never have a chance to fulfill their higher needs, such as relating to other people, having satisfying, meaningful contact with others, having a sense of inclusion and affection and response. We never allow these needs to be satisfied because we deal situationally with needs at the lowest level possible. Maslow says that a satisfied need is not a motivator. When we are in the process of building or buying a new home, we look at everyone's house. When it is finally built or bought, we don't look at houses with the same sense of urgency. The need is met and it is no longer a motivator.

In our motivation system, we often create conditions that satisfy one level and never allow people to move on up. This is what Herzberg is also saying. We create work that does not allow people to satisfy ego needs, to feel that "I'm doing something worthwhile" or that "I have the esteem of people." We do not create conditions wherein people achieve the best that is possible for them to achieve (self-actualization).

My guess is that what children are asked to do is at a very simple level; there is not much chance for them to satisfy their higher needs.

We don't look at how we can alter that situation, how we can allow people a greater investment of themselves so that they can get some growth or challenge out of what they have to do. In a rural society a boy has to work because he knows the family depends on the crops. His attitude toward his work is quite different from that of a boy in an urban family who is asked to make his bed or take out the garbage, whose tasks do not allow him to actualize anything. Parents need to find ways to help their children develop, and job enrichment is important.

Motivation through Objectives

There is a program called management by objectives or teaching by objectives. The notion here is, instead of telling workers "If you

54

do this, you are going to get the rewards and avoid the penalties," that we allow people to set their own goals and objectives and involve them in making decisions. If we let workers participate in the process of goal setting, planning, and decision making, we find there is an improvement in motivation. People are willing to work harder with greater quality or in different directions when they have a chance to influence the situation themselves.

Feedback

Another possibility in motivation is to increase the information or data factor. McClelland (1962:99–112) has done extensive work on achievement motivation. One of the things we know about people who have high achievement motivation is that it makes a real difference in their performance if they get immediate, accurate feedback on how they are doing. However, the type of feedback is important, for people respond defensively and negatively to distorted, evaluative, or judgmental feedback.

Competition

Another way of altering situations is to introduce competition, which sometimes works well. In our culture we are competitively oriented; we like to win. We like challenge. We can sometimes get people to do things if we can say, "Look, that's what people in the other department are doing. We can do better than that."

However, I saw some dangerous overtones from competition among my own children when they were young. We wanted to get them dressed and fed in the morning, and they wanted to sit around and play in or with the food and not get dressed. So we set up a very simple system. "All right, let's see who can get dressed first. Let's see who can get the food down. Come on. Hurray for Mike, he won!" We began to notice a lot of negative effects between the two older boys. They didn't like each other; they developed resentments. We were getting the food down and the clothes on, but we were noticing side effects that we didn't like.

I hear example after example given of people who have used competition as a way of getting other people to perform. To achieve and win is a tremendous motivating force. Boys in athletics compete in teams. They spend tremendous time and energy in competing. I wonder what happens to those who lose. This is a side effect. I remember reading *Peanuts* one time: Schultz's Charlie Brown was telling Linus about his dream. "Boy, I had the greatest dream about a big football game at the homecoming. The home team was behind, six to nothing, and at the last minute the home team threw a long pass, scored a touchdown, and kicked the extra point. Just as the game ended, they won, seven to six, and the crowd went wild."

And Linus said, "I wonder how the other team felt."

In conclusion, in trying to motivate another person, here are some of the strategies that are open: direct influence, altering the situation in some way, getting more feedback, or using competition. Each strategy requires an understanding of self, the people involved, the nature of the system, and the goals one is trying to achieve. Motivation is complex, but with more insight we might be more successful.

References

Allport, Gordon W.
   1937   *Personality: A Psychological Interpretation.* New York: Henry Holt & Co.

Argyris, Chris
   1957   *Personality and Organization.* New York: Harper & Row, Publishers.

Herzberg, Frederick
   1966   *Work and the Nature of Man.* Cleveland: World Publishing Co.

Kelman, Herbert C.
   1961   Process of opinion change. *Public Opinion Quarterly* 25 (Spring):57–78.

McClelland, David
   1962   Business drive and national achievement. *Harvard Business Review* (July-August):99–112.

Maslow, Abraham
   1943   A theory of human motivation. *Psychology Review* 50:370–96.

PERSONAL CONCERN

In a recent survey various groups of organization members were asked this question: "Have you ever had a leader in this organization come to you and ask you such questions as 'How do you really feel about your work, this organization, or your department? How do you feel about the position you hold? What recommendations do you have for improving things in your position that would allow you to grow and develop more thoroughly?'" Approximately five hundred people were asked this question, and only about 25 percent responded in the affirmative. Almost 75 percent indicated that not once in their work experience had they ever had a close, personal visit with any leader to talk about their deep feelings about the organization, their position in the organization, or their recommendations for improvement.

Research Findings

In the field of organization and leadership research, we find that significant differences in people's productivity and morale depend on the attitudes and behavior of their leaders. Consider the following statement from a major research center:

> The high producing supervisors were more employee-oriented and less production-oriented than their low-producing colleagues. The low supervisors emphasized production and technical aspects of the job, and tended to think of their employees as "people to get work done," in contrast to emphasizing training people, taking an interest in employees, and considering them primarily as individual human beings (R. L. Kahn and D. Katz, 1960).

57

Dr. Rensis Likert feels that a fundamental condition for an effective organization is its conformity to what he calls the "principle of supportive relationships." This principle is defined as follows:

> The leadership and other processes of the organization must be such as to ensure a maximum probability that in all interactions and in all relationships within the organization, each member, in the light of his background, values, desires, and expectations, will view the experience as supportive and one which builds and maintains his sense of personal worth and importance (1967: 47).

The challenge for the leader in any organization is to spend the time and to engage in the right kinds of actions that will let those who work with or under him know that he has a vital, personal concern about them as individuals. Each person has a need to feel that those over him in the organization are concerned about him as a unique person and that he is not just a number or a statistic or a category.

Results and Personal Concern

No organization can exist for long unless work is done and goals accomplished. The leader cannot ignore work-centered activities, and he should see that activities are planned, programs are set up, materials are in order, assignments made and followed through. But all of this must be done in the general atmosphere of an overriding concern for those who must do the work and carry out the assignments. When people feel that their superior thinks the work is more important than the people who do the work, the motivation to work is lessened.

This is the critical balance — good planning, organization, and high performance standards for work in an atmosphere where each individual feels confident that he, personally, is understood, appreciated, and highly involved.

There is good evidence that the high-production, work-centered supervisor with low concern for people engages in a self-defeating strategy. The harder he tries to push people to perform, the more resistance he generates, and this often triggers him into a vicious cycle of more pressure and more resistance that spirals endlessly away from the goals that everyone really wants.

Nonpersonal Actions

Often, without realizing it is happening, a leader engages in action that seems to those who experience it that he has low concern for them personally. Following are some kinds of actions that may communicate low concern for the individual and his personal needs:

1. Interviewing for Employment

In the very first contact between employer and employee, teacher and student, boss and subordinate, client and consultant, the discussion may center so strongly on what is expected of the subordinate person as to work performance that there are no indications his superior is concerned about his questions, concerns, fears, or aspirations.

2. Interacting at Work

In the daily interaction of regular work, what is the nature of the contact? Highly work-centered bosses deal primarily, if not exclusively, with concerns about output. This is a legitimate and necessary concern, but the superior who operates from a principle of supportive relationships will be talking with his subordinate at different times about a variety of issues: how he feels about his work, what suggestions he has for improvement, what his plans are for the future, how the boss can help in giving growth and development experiences.

3. Making Assignments and Decisions

The boss with low personal concern often never thinks to get others' inputs, suggestions, or ideas before making a decision or assignment. This lack of involvement suggests to the subordinate that the superior is not interested in him or his resources, or that the boss doesn't respect his thinking. This is not to say that all subordinates must be contacted before any decision can be made, but there are those decisions that directly affect the subordinates in which their inputs can and should legitimately be considered.

4. Letting People Remain Uninformed

A mark of respect and concern for others is to let them know what is happening. When one finds changes made that he never knew about, he feels cheated and somehow betrayed. He asks himself the question, "Why didn't they tell me or let me know this change was coming? Don't they trust me, or am I just too unimportant to worry about?"

5. Handling a Crisis

When a crisis emerges, there is a terrible tendency to forget all about people, particularly if they are the center or the cause of the crisis. Research in the restaurant industry shows that when a waitress was under great pressure (she had dropped a tray of food), she did not need her superior to "chew her out," particularly in front of others. At that moment she needed some support and understanding to help her through a difficult situation.

Barriers to Personal Concern

Why is it that so many people avoid engaging in any type of personal contact, particularly in a work setting? Argyris (1962) has shown from his research that a large majority of managers in organizations do not feel it is appropriate to deal with anything concerning feelings and emotions. To ask subordinates how they *feel* would be a violation of their own expectations of what a good manager should do.

Some people have this antifeeling orientation because they lack needed skills for personal contacts. They do not know how to initiate such contacts, and they would feel very uncomfortable and at a loss if either strong positive or negative feelings emerged. Still others avoid personal concern because of real or imagined time constraints. It does take time to create a climate of warmth, talk in depth, explore feelings and reactions. Work schedules may make such a contact difficult unless it is seen as a high-priority matter.

How to Develop Personal Concern

What can be done by leaders to create an atmosphere of personal concern and individual acceptance, in addition to rectifying the above problems?

1. Taking Time

Too often the interaction around a work activity is hurried, poorly timed, and conducted with the feeling "we're both busy, so let's hurry and get this over with." Making an assignment, request, or interview should be scheduled with time enough to express real appreciation, to find out any personal concerns, and to talk about not only the job but also the person.

2. Asking the Concerned Question

For many reasons, people shy away from talking personally with others. It seems safer to "talk business." But one can move into the area of personal concern saying something like this, "I honestly would like to know how you feel about the department and your work assignment. If you have any qualms or reservations, I would like to know, and if you have any suggestions for improving things, they would be most welcome." Or one might say, "How are things going for you now? Are you having any problems, questions, or difficulties with which I can help?" It may be possible to open up a discussion of something you, the leader, have noticed that you feel may be bothering the other person.

3. Listening with Understanding

If a person begins to talk about his real feelings of concern about matters that truly affect him, the leader must *listen* and try to understand. It will not be helpful if the leader invites sharing and then interrupts with such comments as, "That's not how it really is," or "You didn't really get a clear picture of what we are trying to do," or "Let me tell you what I would do if I were you," or "I don't see how you could have that kind of reaction."

Listening with understanding or empathy is the process of honestly trying to see the problem of the situation from the other person's position, to understand how and why he sees and responds to things the way he does, so that help can be given from where he is rather than from where the leader is.

4. Being Willing to Do Something

One of the most common reactions of the leader after a person has shared a real concern is to ask, "How can I help?" This question often puts the person who has shared in a real dilemma. He may not have been asking for help, and he probably doesn't know what would be appropriate. He feels awkward and embarrassed and says, "Oh, I don't need any help," or "I don't know what you could do."

Instead of asking *what* he can do, the leader should do something: he can take action. He can express understanding, concern, and empathy. He can respond with an expression of appreciation or gratitude or a touch or a pat on the back. He can suggest action, such as, "I know it is a difficult problem; let me go with you to see the situation for myself"; or "Let's sit down and plan exactly what would be the best action to take."

If one has real concern, he can almost always do something that shows his concern is real — not just a ploy he is using because he read an article on personal concern and felt he ought to try it.

References

Argyris, Chris
  1962 *Interpersonal Competence and Organization Effectiveness.* Homewood, Ill.: Irwin-Dorsey.

Dubin, Robert, et al.
  1965 *Leadership and Productivity.* San Francisco: Chandler Publishing Co.

Kahn, Robert L., and D. Katz
  1960 Leadership practices in relation to productivity and morale. *Group Dynamics.* Evanston: Row-Peterson and Company.

Likert, Rensis
  1967 *The Human Organization.* New York: McGraw-Hill.

ADJUSTMENT

Whenever people come together to combine their efforts in some type of interaction to produce results or achieve goals, the possibility of differences or conflicts occurs. People differ in many ways: they have different experiences, backgrounds, attitudes, personalities, values, goals, and life-styles. Such differences can erupt into conflicts that erode relationships and make the achievement of goals difficult unless people learn to make appropriate adjustments.

Role theory allows us to outline and understand more clearly the forms of adjustment that people make when differences occur.

Role Expectations

Each person enters a relationship with certain ideas about his own behavior and certain expectations about the behavior of the other person. Role expectations are the ways one person feels another should behave. Thus, at least two sets of expectations are involved in every relationship — one set for each person, for each has expectations of himself and the other.

The problem that usually arises is that role definitions are at variance with role performance. There is often a difference between what someone else thinks one should do and what one actually does. It is this disparity — between what one persons thinks should be done and what the other actually does — that creates strain in a relationship. The differences people have in their expectations are the source of much misunderstanding and failure in relationships. If what the boss expects of a subordinate differs from what the subordinate thinks he ought to do, there will be a high possibility that a violation of the boss's expectations will occur with the resulting penalties or problems. This is especially likely if the boss has not spent adequate time in clearly defining his expectations to the subordinate. Failure to clarify expectations is an important element in causing differences between expectations and performance, as illustrated in the following example:

> Jerry can't understand what is happening. For the past two weeks it seems he can never do anything right. His boss, Tim Hartley, is on him all the time, but he doesn't know why. Jerry feels he is trying to do a good job. He tries to stay out of Mr. Hartley's way and can do his own work without bothering anyone. He is in the process of moving ahead to prove that he is a good employee — one who takes the initiative, does not have to rely on the boss for everything, shows results even if others aren't doing a good job. But for some reason that doesn't seem to be enough.
>
> Tim Hartley is also perplexed. He likes Jerry and feels that he is a valuable employee, but he is also a problem. Tim thinks to himself, "Why won't he ever come and check things out before he moves ahead on his own? This could keep me informed and keep him from making some unnecessary mistakes. Also, a good employee fits into the team, and he is always working by himself, showing other employees up and creating a lot of resentment."

What to do? Here clearly is a case of mismatched role expectations. Jerry expects himself to behave in certain ways consistent with his definition of a "good" worker. His boss has quite another notion of a good worker and expects Jerry to behave differently than he does now. Unfortunately neither clearly understands the expectations of the other.

Sanctions

Sanctions are the rewards or punishments administered by one person to the other to the degree the other meets or fails to meet role expectations. If the subordinate's performance in his role meets the boss's role expectations, he will generally apply positive sanctions or rewards, such as praise, recognition, and good will. If the role performance violates his expectations, he will often apply negative sanctions: criticism, withdrawal of trust, or demotions. Tim Hartley, in the case above, is already applying negative sanctions to Jerry.

Generally human interactions move along most smoothly if the following conditions exist:

1. The parties interacting have a high level of agreement on norms and personal preferences.

2. The parties involved agree on mutual role definitions and role expectations.

3. The role performance of one is in agreement with the role expectations of the other, and positive sanctions are the end result of the interaction.

Interpersonal Adjustment

We may now consider the process of making adjustments in interpersonal relationships:

Points of Conflict

Conflicts in the work situation may arise for the following reasons:

1. If the norms and personal preferences of the boss are in conflict with those of the subordinate.

2. If the role performance of the subordinate does not agree with the role expectations of the boss.

3. If the role performance of the boss does not agree with the role expectations of the subordinate.

In each of the above cases dissatisfaction with the relationship may occur with a resulting application of negative sanctions. Negative sanctions may be directly or indirectly applied, or these feelings of dissatisfaction may be repressed or directed toward someone or something else.

The case of Tim Hartley and Jerry shows what happens when the role performance of the subordinate does not agree with the expectations of the boss. Jerry is behaving as consistently as possible with what he feels are the requirements for a good subordinate, but this will never be adequate unless his boss alters his expectations. As the boss applies negative sanctions (criticism, yelling, "being on" Jerry), he begins to violate Jerry's expectations about how a boss should behave. Jerry feels that a good boss will not criticize unjustly or without explaining. If the boss continues his pressure, Jerry may react in negative ways. In fact, he is already starting to avoid the boss. The situation can build up in a cycle of negative action and reaction until a crisis occurs. Open conflict may result.

The norms and personal preferences of the boss, which he has inadequately explained to Jerry, are in conflict with Jerry's. Jerry, unaware of the conflict, assumes that he is doing what any reasonable boss would want him to do. Their mutual lack of clarification has caused the problem with role expectation and performance.

Possible Methods of Adjustment

In each of the above conflict situations, there are certain kinds of adjustments available:

In situation 1, the boss and the subordinate need to clarify to each other their norms or personal preferences so that each understands the point of view of the other. This of necessity involves mature and extensive communication. To the degree that the disparity between norms is translated into role performance, as in situations 2 and 3 above, the following adjustments would be applicable:

1. The subordinate (or boss) can change his role performance completely to meet the role expectations of the other.

2. The subordinate (or boss) can change his role expectations completely to coincide with the role performance of the other.

3. There can be a mutual adjustment, each one altering some. The subordinate alters his role performance to a degree, and the boss alters his role expectations to a similar degree, so that role performance and role expectations are compatible. In each of the above cases the end result is agreement between role performance and role expectations.

What are the possible adjustments available to Jerry and his boss? Assuming that one or the other initiates a discussion where their mismatched expectations are disclosed, and assuming that they want to work out an adjustment, the following are possibilities:

1. Jerry, upon learning of his boss's expectations, could say, "Now that I know what you expect, I'll really try to do what you want."

2. Tim Hartley could say, "Jerry, I'm glad I found out how you prefer to work. I'll try to put you in work settings so you can draw from your strengths and perform the way you do best."

3. Each could alter some. Jerry could agree to keep Tim better informed and to clear plans with him before taking independent action. Tim could agree to give Jerry new freedom to let him work in situations not requiring much team effort and to let Jerry know promptly if things are not going well.

There is another type of adjustment possible. In some cases the two, recognizing a disparity between role performance and role expectations or between norms, and acknowledging that change is difficult or impossible, could "agree to disagree." In such cases each recognizes and respects the position of the other without accepting or adjusting to it. This pattern of agreeing to disagree is not an adjustment in the same sense as those listed above. The "adjustment" comes from the agreement by both persons that a certain area is "out of bounds" as far as the application of sanctions is concerned. There is no change in behavior but some change in expectations: Each now expects that certain subjects will not be raised as issues and that no sanctions will be applied over them. This type of adjustment may be possible in certain areas of work life, but some areas may be so vital to the relationship that in them one of the other types of adjustment will have to be reached.

Some Problems in Adjustment

Public vs. Private Adjustment

The discussion about the example of Jerry and Tim emphasizes the actual, outward, public behavior of the persons as the essence of adjustment. Complete adjustment would be obtained only if the change in behavior were accompanied by a mental state of "feeling good" about it. If Jerry changed his role performance to meet his boss's expectations publicly, adjustment would appear to occur, but privately he could resent "giving in" to him and transfer this resentment into areas other than that around which the "adjustment" took place.[1]

The Need for Feedback

A necessary element in the process of changing social behavior is that of feedback. It is difficult, if not impossible, for one person to know exactly how he is violating the expectations of another if the other does not respond with adequate feedback. Often feedback cues given out by one person may be misread, misinterpreted, or denied if the feedback is not stated clearly in an atmosphere of acceptance and in a climate that is not "defensive" (Gibb, 1959). Open communication of expectations and feedback about the degree to which someone has met, or failed to meet, these expectations is often extremely difficult. There is fear that "if I give feedback to him, I may lose what warmth and goodwill we now have," or fear that the other may retaliate. A person may likewise be inhibited from giving feedback by his feelings of inadequacy about how to proceed, the lack of an appropriate time, or his feelings that he is not really sure he is "right" about his own criticism of the other person.

Often one learns of the expectations of others and how he has or has not met them only via a trial-and-error method or in a sudden outburst of feeling when the other feels, "I can't take it any longer." Neither of these conditions for feedback encourages the opportunity for mutual sharing of data in an atmosphere of cooperation where the feedback has the best opportunity of being perceived as being helpful to the total relationship.

---

[1] In testing a similar phenomenon, Kelman (1956) distinguishes between *compliance* (the adopting of a new behavior not because one believes in its content, but because he expects to gain specific rewards of approval and avoid specific punishments or disapproval); *identification* (the adopting of new behavior because it is associated with the desired relationship); and *internalization* (the adopting of a new behavior because one finds it useful for the solution of a problem or because it is congenial to his needs).

Adjustment vs. Reconciliation

Adjustment has been discussed in terms of bringing into agreement the behavior of one person with the expectations of another, accompanied by a feeling of acceptance of the modified behavior by the one who makes the adjustment. A phenomenon recognized in many cases of discord is the subsequent process of "reconciliation." This is usually a process of repairing the feeling of unity and cohesion.

From an examination of a number of case studies (Dyer, 1965) it appears entirely possible for people to be reconciled without achieving any adjustment in the sense described above. A violation of expectations often results in a feeling of discord and hostility between two people. In a moment of mutual sympathy and regret for past actions, they may express regret and apologies which put them back in a harmonious relationship with each other, but since no modification of either expectation or behavior has occurred, disruption may recur at any time.

It is also possible for a type of adjustment to occur without a repair of the emotional state of unity. People could meet each other's expectations and still not feel good about their behavior.

In terms of reinforcement learning theory it seems essential that a modification of either expectations or behavior on the part of one person be rewarded by the other (Miller and Dollard, 1941). One needs to find out not only what one does wrong, but also what one does right. The continuous giving of positive sanctions may be a necessary part of adjustment.

Cautions

1. This chapter is a logical outline of adjustment possibilities in a particular frame of reference. It does not pretend to cover the socio-psychological dynamics involved in the difficult process of attitude or behavior change. One should never presume that such adjustments are psychologically easy.

The argument has been that all conflict is a result of one person's behavior not meeting another's expectations or vice versa. The correction of such conflict is often more complex, for one's behavior and/or expectations may be related to one's "personality," including certain temperament factors, conceptions of self, important self-other needs, and the like. The changing of one's role behavior or expectations may demand personal adjustments that are extremely difficult. One's level of maturity will also be an important factor in determining his capability to make adjustments.

2. The above outline does not suggest which type of conflict is most frequent or which type of adjustment is easiest. More research is needed in the area of adjustment using this schema. It is, however, a commonly held position that it is easier to change one's role ex-

pectations than to change another's behavior. It would, for example, probably be easier for Tim Hartley to modify his own expectations about Jerry than for him to expect Jerry to change his pattern of activity that has resulted from years of experience, training, and attitudes.

3. It should be noted that there are other methods available for the *reduction* of conflict in work situations without actually *adjusting* in the sense defined above; that is, the people involved make some alteration of norms, roles, or role expectations. This avenue generally is the alteration of the *situation* that may be fostering certain role behaviors or expectations. For example, if conflict occurs between a boss and a subordinate because the subordinate spends too much time on nonessential matters (as seen by the boss — behavior thus violating his expectations), a change in job assignment may put the subordinate in an entirely new situation resulting in new, more acceptable behavior. This is one possible solution to the problem between Jerry and Tim. Jerry could be put under a different boss or in a different work situation so that he could work on his own.

Conclusion

No one should pretend that adjustments are ever easy. Sometimes just making expectations known will clear up problems almost immediately. In other situations adjustment will require effort, patience, and understanding, as people try to change patterns they have built up over a lifetime.

References

Dyer, William G., and Dick Urban
  1962 Analyzing marital adjustment using role theory. *Marriage and Family Living* 20 (November): 53–58.

Cutler, Beverly R., and William G. Dyer
  1965 Initial adjustment processes in young married couples. *Social Forces* 44, no. 2 (December): 195–201.

Gibb, Jack R.
  1959 Factors Producing Defensive Behavior with Groups, VI. Final Technical Report, Office of Naval Research, Nont — 2285 (01).

Kahn, Robert L., et al.
  1964 *Organizational Stress*, especially part 6, Conflict and Attempted Solution. New York: John Wiley and Son.

Kelman, Herbert C.
  1956 Three processes of acceptance of social influence: Compliance, identification, and internalization. Paper read at the meetings of the American Psychological Association, Chicago, Illinois (August 30).

Miller, Neal, and John Dollard
  1941 *Social Learning and Imitation*. New Haven: Yale University Press.

Tannenbaum, Arnold S.
  1966 *Social Psychology of the Work Organization*, especially chapter 4, Personal adjustment and conflict in the work organization. Belmont, Calif.: Wadsworth Publishing Company.

PLANNED CHANGE

Almost everyone would like to be an expert in planned change at one time or another. We are often in a position where we would consciously like to produce change in certain conditions or people. Parents sometimes want their children to change their behavior, and teachers, bosses, ministers, and administrators desire at times to see change or improvement in the performance of students, members, or workers. Managers in organizations sometimes long for an upturn in profits, quality of product, amount of service, or amount of production. And usually, if the need for change is strong enough, we try to do something to stimulate, encourage, direct, or influence the desired changes to occur. What kinds of change strategies actually work, and which lead us into unproductive pathways?

Force Field Analysis

During World War II, the government of the United States became interested in an area of change. At that time meat was rationed, and scarce ration stamps were required to secure the choice cuts of meats — roasts, steaks, and chops. Other cuts of meat were not rationed (liver, brain, tongue, heart), but for a variety of reasons people would not use them. Kurt Lewin, a professor at the University of Iowa, was asked to do some research on planned change. The issue: Was it possible to get housewives to change their meat-buying and eating habits and to start using these nonrationed products? With his research assistants, Lewin set up some experimental conditions. Some housewives were put in groups that listened to "attractive

71

lectures . . . which linked the problem of nutrition with the war effort, emphasized the vitamin and mineral value of the [nonrationed] meats. . . . Both the health and economic aspects were stressed. The preparation of these meats was discussed in detail. . . . Mimeographed recipes were distributed" (Lewin, 1958). Yet despite all these extensive efforts, only 3 percent of the women who heard the lectures served any of the nonrationed cuts of meats.

Other housewives were asked to participate in discussion groups and were requested to discuss food, nutrition, and the war effort — to see what housewives could do to assist in this area. Following the discussion sessions it was found that 32 percent of the women served at least one of the previously avoided products. Apparently something happened in the group sessions that was not present in the lectures to produce change. Lewin's own analysis indicates he felt the differences were due to (1) the degree of involvement of people in the discussion and decision, (2) the motivation in actually being a party to the decision, and (3) group influence and support of others in reinforcing the decision.

From this and other similar research, Lewin developed a model for analyzing the planned-change process. He visualized any existing condition as in a state of balance or equilibrium (with some fluctuation) locked between two sets of forces — driving and restraining. He called his model of counterbalancing forces "force field analysis."

In Lewin's meat-eating problem, the restraining forces that kept housewives from buying and using the nonrationed meats seemed to be taste, smell, appearance, family reactions, low status attached to eating these meats, lack of approval by others, and lack of information about preparation. Driving forces that pushed toward change were patriotism, hunger, nutrition, no stamps needed, new experience. Apparently drive was not enough to overcome the strength of the resistance.

Force Fie'd Analysis — Model of an Existing Condition

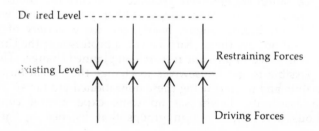

De ired Level - - - - - - - - - - - - - - - - - - -

Restraining Forces

Existing Level

Driving Forces

Change Strategies

Given the field-of-forces model, there are really three basic change strategies:
1. *Increase* the driving forces.
2. *Decrease* the restraining forces.
3. Do both.

There is good evidence to suggest that just increasing the driving forces results in a certain degree of increased resistance, and it may not maintain the change unless pressure is constantly applied. According to Lewin, change occurs when the existing situation could be "unfrozen," moved to a new level, and then "refrozen" at the new position. Just applying more pressure does not seem adequate to get the change fixed or refrozen at the new level.

More appropriate is the strategy of either reducing or eliminating restraints, or even better, moving previously restraining forces around to the driving side. In the meat-eating case, the lecture made an effort to put more pressures on — appealing to patriotism, helping the war effort, and trying to reduce the one restraint of lack of preparation knowledge by passing out recipes.

The group discussion–decision method changed peer-group pressure from a restraining force to a driving force. Women who formerly had been uneasy about the reactions of their peers were now getting support from those very peers. Even the group-process method was not strong enough to overcome the resistance forces, for more than 65 percent of the women still would not use the undesirable cuts of meat.

Force Field Analysis and Action Research

In more recent years a systematic method for planning change has emerged. It is called *action research* and can be related to Lewin's earlier model. Action research involves the following steps and follows what would need to be done if one were to utilize Lewin's model:

1. Define the Problem and Determine the Change Goals

In planned change one moves from the existing situation, which is seen as a "problem" or a condition to be altered. The change target or goal is also identified. Lewin's model suggests the same beginning.

2. Gather the Data

In order to determine what the *real* forces in the situation are, it is important to gather accurate information about both resistance forces and positive factors. If possible, it is helpful to learn which forces are most critical and which are amenable to change. Some factors may be open to change but are really not important, and some very important forces may be outside the ability of people to influence to any great degree. Data gathering may be accomplished by interviews, questionnaires, instruments, or direct observations in which the data about the forces in the situation are collected. However it is done, the results are fed back into the system as the basis for achieving change.

3. Summarize and Analyze the Data

After being accumulated, the data are put into some type of summary form. For larger amounts of data, sophisticated computer and statistical analyses may be necessary. For interviews or direct observations, dominant "themes" or issues mentioned by several respondants should be identified. Analysis of the data should help determine which factors are most important, which are amenable to change, which cannot be influenced or modified, and which have the greatest probability for lending themselves to a successful change endeavor.

4. Plan the Action

Following analysis of the data, the plan of action to be utilized is prepared. In a good action plan the following matters are considered:
  a. Who are the significant people who need to support a change program?
  b. Where should action taking begin?
  c. Who should be assigned to take what specific action?
  d. When should first reports of action be prepared for review?
  e. What resources (time, money, equipment, personnel) are needed for the change program?
  f. What is the estimated completion time?

5. Take Action

After the plan of action has been carefully worked out, the next logical step is to put the plan into effect. Lewin's model would encourage the following in the action-taking stage:
  a. Work on reducing restraining forces.
  b. Involve people in planning their own change.
  c. Develop social supports for change.
  d. Get people to make their own decisions to change.

6. Evaluate

Any good action research program has built into it the criteria for its own success. How do you know if you have reached your goals? Goals should be stated in such a way that evaluation criteria are evident and easily applied. For example, if an organization stated its change goal as "improve communications," its success would be very difficult to measure. Any increase in talking could be said to "improve communications." A more measurable goal would be one like this: "Have every manager conduct a sharing and evaluation session with each of his subordinates every three months." Measurement is possible to see if this change goal has been achieved. If not, recycling the action-research model must be initiated: gathering new data, analyzing it, and repeating the whole process.

Conditions of Successful Change

In planning a change program, it would be well to check the change plan against the findings of Gene Dalton (1970). He reviewed most of the literature on personal and organizational change and identified the following six conditions associated with successful change efforts:

1. There was a strongly felt need, tension, or "hurt" that moved people to want to change.

2. The person assisting in change was highly esteemed by the persons involved in changing.

3. The change effort moved from general proposals to specific plans and workable subgoals.

4. The change plan increased the self-esteem of the people who were changing.

5. The change plan resulted in new social ties or reformulation of old ties around new behaviors and attitudes.

6. The people changing shifted from an external motive for changing to an internal understanding and commitment.

The change plan should include as many of the above elements as are feasible, given the conditions surrounding the change effort.

Change and Anxiety

An important consideration in implementing a change plan is coping with the anxiety that results, particularly when the initiation of the change at first results in an even less productive effort. Early research by Coch and French (1948) found that even under the best of change conditions, when workers are asked to change assignments and begin new, unfamiliar work, their production falls off. This dropoff in performance is usually accompanied by an increase in anxiety on the part of those who began the change program: an anxiety gap (see diagram) develops.

At the point of heightened anxiety and decreasing performance, there is a terrible tendency to want to cancel out the whole change

Anxiety Gap

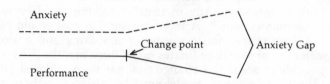

effort and return to the earlier state; for, as bad as it was, it seems better than the new condition. There are times when a change program is not well conceived and should be cancelled, but if it has been based on data, the people changing have been involved in choosing the change, plans have been thought through, and people are committed to them, the major issue is to manage the anxiety — not the change. The Coch-French study found that in motor skill performance it takes about two weeks for a turnaround in performance to occur. In some other areas it may take many months before improvement is noticeable. One manages his anxiety best by talking honestly about his concerns, reviewing the progress and the plans, and making additional modifications as needed. No one can guarantee the success of every change program. There will always be elements of risk and surprise and sometimes failure. One plans for change because action seems a better course than inaction. If the plan is well conceived, initiated, and carried out, the chances for success seem better than the slow erosion of a deteriorating situation where nothing is done.

References

Bennis, Warren G., Kenneth Benne, and Robert Chin
    1969 *Planning and Change.* New York: Holt, Rinehart and Winston, Inc.

Coch, Lester, and John R. P. French
    1948 Overcoming resistance to change. *Human Relations.* 512–32.

Dalton, Gene, Paul Lawrence, and Laurence Greiner
    1970 *Organizational Changes and Development.* Homewood, Ill.: Irwin-Dorsey.

Lewin, Kurt
    1958 Group decision and social change. In *Readings in Social Psychology*, ed. Macoby, Newcomb, and Hartly. New York: Henry Holt and Company, 197–212.

Lippitt, Ronald, Jeanne Watson, and Bruce Westley
    1958 *Dynamics of Planned Change.* New York: Harcourt Brace and World, Inc.

GROUP BEHAVIOR

A hard-core fact of our society is that most activities in which we engage are within the context of a functioning group. There is ample evidence that most organizations are made up of interlocking groups, and a key skill for managers in systems is to learn to manage groups, not individuals only.

Argyris (1957) has pointed out that children in our culture start out at an immature state — dependent, subordinate, submissive, conforming, and using only a few surface skills. What we profess to desire for these children is to see them achieve a level of maturity where they are finally independent and creative, have leadership potential, initiate action, and utilize all their skills. It is Argyris's thesis that the types of groups and organizations into which we funnel people tend to maintain them at the original level of immaturity.

If we look at many of our schools, social clubs, religious groups, and later on our industrial and business groups, we find that if a person is to get along best in them he remains submissive, obedient and conforming, dependent, and is encouraged to use only a few of his skills. If, however, as often happens, the individual realizes he has unused potential, he may become frustrated, angry, hostile, withdrawn, rebellious — or, in other words, "disturbed." We centralize authority, control, and rewards in these organizations and tend to foster dependency, conformity, and obedience by having people compete with each other for these rewards. In families, schools, and work groups, when the authority is centralized in the parents, teachers, or bosses, what kind of behavior do we reward? Parents idealize the child that is "well-behaved." Similarly, teachers like the child who "does what he is told." Managers often appreciate most the hard-working conformist. Anxiety is created together with possible frustration and hostility when the person is faced with reward or lack of reward. Employers have economic sanction, but parents and friends have the greater weapon — *affection*. The individual may continue to act in ways we describe as "childish" and "immature," when in fact his total social development has not shown him or allowed him to act any other way. Let us spell out in more detail some of the dimensions of group action, which if followed characterize a "healthy" group that in turn produces healthy, mature individuals.

The Group-Standard Dimension

All groups set standards affecting the behavior of their members. Sometimes these standards are unrealistic, and people work under constant pressure trying to meet them. In some families the standard for the children is to be like the oldest boy or girl. Younger children sometimes go through life trying to measure up to an unfortunate choice of standards. Consider the college student who took five classes in which each professor established the standard of two hours of homework for each hour in class. This was a physically unrealistic standard, and as you probably know, students have ways of dealing with such conditions. They defend themselves by copying each other's work, cheating on exams, sharing assignments, trading book reports — and the list goes on.

I worked with one group of professional people who were having real difficulty meeting the standards they had established for themselves in a project. It was a volunteer project that they were carrying out in addition to other duties. After some very probing meetings, they finally saw that for a few leaders of the project the group's standards and goals were the most important matters on which they were working. For most of the others, however, this project ranked about fourth or fifth in importance compared with other commitments. The leaders were pressuring for a set of standards that were unrealistic for the others. Finally they worked out common standards of performance, time, and expense on which they could all agree and work without feelings of guilt and pressure.

If a person does not achieve the standards set by the group, his self-esteem suffers. He may have real feelings of inadequacy or guilt. New members of any work unit may run into standards of work and excellence for which they are unprepared, and they suffer from their inadequacies. Groups need constantly to examine their standards to see if they are realistic in terms of the resources of the group members.

Groups also have at their command a kind of awesome power to induce members to conform to their standards. Members are rewarded by being accepted, included, and praised if they abide by the group norms but are rejected, excluded, and ridiculed if they do not conform. How wonderful to be warmly accepted and included by others, and how terrible to be an outcast — rejected and ridiculed!

Standards which allow acceptance or rejection often have no, objective validity. One work group rejected new workers because they came from a different ethnic background from those in the majority. In one high school the standard for acceptance in the girls' cliques was the wearing of Jantzen skirts and sweaters. No other kind would do. Some girls stood in a circle at the main entrance, and as other girls would come in, they would check the label in the neck of each sweater to see if it were a Jantzen. If it were, its wearer was accepted. If not, she was not included in the circle. Some of the poorer girls went to the home economics teacher and asked if she would cut the labels from her Jantzen sweaters so they could sew them in their sweaters and thus win acceptance. I wonder how many people there are who suffer from frustration, feelings of rejection, and feelings of inadequacy because for one reason or another they cannot measure up to various group standards equally as arbitrary as those of the girls.

The Involvement Dimension

The essence of the involvement principle is that people work most productively and happily when they are involved in establishing their own goals and procedures. When all group members work together with a high degree of involvement in setting up what they are to do and how they are to do it, they have a sense of commitment not present when goals are imposed on them.

The late Kurt Lewin found that in decision making, when the group as a whole made the decision to have the group members change their method of operation, the results were from two to ten times more effective than when groups were asked to make changes as a result of lectures exhorting them to change.

In industry the results are striking. When groups are given the responsibility for their own goals and procedures, productivity and morale are increased.

Groups are often caught in an interesting dilemma in this matter of involvement in setting their own goals. On one hand, people like to be involved and to participate in planning for their own actions. On the other hand, when they are not used to doing this, or they run into conflict with people who have slightly different goals, or they cannot agree on procedures, it is often easier to rely on an authority who will tell them what to do and how to do it. Then it is the authority's responsibility to keep after them to do the job, and it's his problem if the work doesn't get done. When we constantly turn to authorities to do this work for us, dependency is reinforced. When people are not involved, they can belong to a group for years and never really participate. An essential skill for leaders is the ability to build real involvement and participation in group members.

The Authority-of-Leadership Dimension

Almost all formal groups and many informal ones have a recognized leader who represents something of a higher status, superior position, or greater power. It is important to see how these leaders function in the group and how the group members relate to them.

In connection with the so-called aggressive person, we need to explore more fully the effects of group organization in producing aggressive action. Research has shown that when children who were aggressive in a group with one leadership style — namely authoritarian — were shifted to a group with a different leadership style — that of a democratic nature — the degree of aggressiveness in these children decreased markedly. Aggression should not be seen merely as a personality trait. It — together with the whole personality — must be seen as it operates within a particular type of group structure.

One study showed that the type of leadership pattern set by the teacher affected the behavior of the students. If the teacher were dominant in her contacts with the students, the students showed more compliance with, as well as rejection of, the teacher's domination. Also in these cases the students were more easily distracted from schoolwork, presumably because they spent more time worrying about the teacher than about the accomplishment of the work. Where the teacher was primarily helpful and tried to integrate the students into class activities, there was more spontaneity, initiative, voluntary social helping of student by student, and more effective problem solving.

Along this same line, another study showed that better classroom attitudes exist when the students have greater opportunity to express their own ideas and feelings. The teachers would more often ask questions about the student's feelings and would praise, encourage, and accept the student's ideas and feelings in a nonthreatening way. Those classrooms with a less desirable feeling found the teacher spending most of the time lecturing, giving directions and criticism. I am sure that these findings in the classroom are true of many other groups.

Commonly people relate to the authority person in one of three ways: Either they are very dependent on the leader, are hostile or counterdependent, or are interdependent, that is, they can work with the leader in a cooperative way. Some leaders like people to be dependent and encourage this; some leaders are so task oriented they do not see the counterreactions that drain off the energies and creativity and emotional well-being of the members. Hopefully those in leadership positions center their focus on the people and their needs and try to create conditions which allow the leaders to work *with* them rather than *over* them.

The Feedback Dimension

Here we draw a term from the field of engineering. Feedback in a guided missile is the process whereby electronic computers guiding the missile detect when the missile is going off course and feed data back into the direction device which allows the missile to return to the right track.

Groups and individuals need to have a similar type of mechanism — that is, some way of finding out when they are behaving in ways that are seen as "off the track" so they can find out what they need to do to get back on the right course again.

It is not easy either to give or to receive feedback. People are reluctant to tell others their mistakes, as in the bad breath ad which states that "even your best friends won't tell you." Also, people who are told they are "off the track" often react in very defensive ways, for they need to protect themselves. A common reaction when someone tells us our errors is to attack him and point out all his faults.

Groups need to develop the kind of climate or atmosphere in which feedback can be expressed with the real understanding that it is given in a helpful way. More groups need to have some way of looking at what they are doing and getting some evaluation and feedback on how the group is working. Individuals and groups can err. If they are to improve, they need to know their errors in such a way that they are not damaged but helped. Feedback is discussed in greater depth in other chapters.

The Climate or Atmosphere Dimension

Emotional climate or atmosphere is both real and difficult to measure. We do know that people are affected dramatically by the emotional milieu within which they must live. We talk most often about the permissive or accepting climate in contrast to the defensive or rejecting climate. We have all been in situations where the climate or prevailing mood of the group could be described as cold or formal or fun or reflective or sad. We've all been in a group or with a group where everything seemed to go right. It's such a good feeling that we hate to see the meeting or activity come to a close.

What are some ingredients that go into creating the type of climate that produces such healthy well-being? I have already mentioned some of the factors: adequate and helpful group standards, involvement of the total group in the problem at hand, leaders who work *with*, not *over*, and a healthy feedback system. Here are some other things to consider.

81

Accepting People Different from Ourselves

We are not all cut from the same cloth, and we need to learn
to accept others for what they have to contribute. Acceptance of
others does not mean we have to like everyone on an intimate basis.
We can learn to appreciate others and their ideas even though they
are quite different from ourselves. In one study, a group of managers
was asked first, "Who do you like best in the organization?" They
listed their choices. Then they were asked, "Who has the best ideas
in the organization?" As we might suspect, they listed the same
choices. I'm sure that most of us really know that the people we like
are not all brilliant, creative, sensitive, and so on. But how often do
we let our feelings of liking distort our perceptions of the worth of
other persons?

Showing Real, Not Pretended, Interest

Some interesting studies have shown that people can readily detect persons who are sincerely interested in others in contrast to persons who are only pretending an interest. We have all shuddered at the hearty "Well, how are we today?" given up by doctors, salesmen, and others who assume a professional but not a real interest. In one study of a hospital ward the patients were asked with whom they talked over their important problems. The professional staff were greatly surprised when the patients listed such persons as the janitor, the elevator boy, one's mother, the patient in the next bed. In the seventy-five interviews made, there was not a single mention of a nurse or one of the professional people working with the patients.

People can tell if others really accept them and are interested in them. Data also show that people can *learn* to be more accepting of others.

Giving Honest Approval and Disapproval

People like to work and live in situations where they are approved for work well done and told honestly and fairly when work is below par. Too often we assume that people we are close to — family, friends, colleagues — know that we approve of and like them. I am interested in the number of times I hear about wives who ask, "Dear, do you really love me? You never tell me." A usual answer is "You ought to know I love you. I married you, didn't I?" I am constantly amazed, as I talk with young people, how many of them are not really sure that their parents love them.

In giving praise and criticism we have to be careful about the use of the so-called sandwich technique. This is the slipping of a piece of criticism between two slices of praise. "John, you did a real fine job last week, *but*, I want to talk to you about what you did yesterday." What this does is keep the praise from having any impact. Every time the employee hears praise, he begins to stiffen for the blow he knows will come. Many managers could improve conditions in their organizations if they could more consistently give honest concern and approval.

Listening Instead of Always Telling

We are all aware that communication is part telling and part listening, but often our listening skills are very low.

Allowing People to Make Mistakes

In a defensive climate people usually spend their time trying to defend themselves against the authority persons. They do not have time or emotional energy to be creative — to grow and mature — for their energies are dissipated in trying to protect themselves from the punishing, censoring, telling, controlling efforts of others. To the degree we can create an accepting, allowing group atmosphere, we will be moving toward the direction of improving the emotional health and maturity of the individual.

The Task-Feeling–Level Dimension

One of the most significant findings of research on groups has been the recognition of two levels of group action. Most groups meet together for a particular task or problem-solving purpose. A task force formed to work out a new policy or program has a specific task to accomplish. But we have also discovered that people, like machines, cannot work indefinitely on a task without some maintenance. People may become tired, angry, frustrated, apathetic, tense, and so forth while they are working together on a problem. Too often in groups we try to ignore all these feelings and needs that are in a state of disrepair and to move all the more quickly to finishing the task before the group blows up. The assumption is that just getting the group to agree on the action to be taken is all that is needed. But we know that, if the feeling level has been neglected and people do not feel happy about the group and its work, they are ineffective in carrying out their assignments, they stay away from meetings, and they are tremendously relieved when the committee finally disbands.

It is *not* a waste of time for groups to take time to ensure that misunderstandings are cleared, to relieve tension, visit and relax, tell jokes, and exchange personal experiences. These are some of the maintenance functions which keep the group in a state of health so it can accomplish its task. We live in a task-oriented society where the emphasis is on more and more production, but we neglect the feelings and emotions of people at our own peril.

These are some of the important dimensions of group life that have serious implications for individual development and mental health. The groups we belong to are major determining forces in shaping our likes and dislikes, establishing our goals and our methods for achieving them, determining what prejudices and attitudes we should hold, and shaping our overall maturity and health. We need to tap the resources of group life for our continuing benefit.

References

Argyris, Chris
 1957 *Personality and Organization.* New York: Harper and Row, Publishers.

Jacobs, Alfred, and Wilford Spradlin
 1974 *The Group as Agent of Change.* New York: Behavioral Publications.

Schein, Edgar, and Warren Bennis
 1965 *Personal and Organization Change through Group Methods.* New York: John Wiley & Sons.

DIAGNOSING SYSTEMS

Planning for change is a constant need in any organization. There are always certain conditions, results, and consequences that managers in the organization are trying to modify in one way or another. These conditions to be changed (hereafter referred to as *output variables*) are such factors as profit/loss, production, costs, wastage, absenteeism, turnover, apathy, involvement, quality, and so on. Whenever one of these conditions varies in an undesirable direction, steps are usually taken to try to improve things. The steps one takes to improve such outputs result from the diagnosis one has made about the factors responsible for the drop-off in the output variable. The adequacy of one's diagnostic ability — thinking appropriately in terms of cause and effect — will make a significant difference in the appropriateness of action taken which in turn will influence output.

If the diagnosis is poor, it is probable that the action designed to improve output factors will result in inadequate change in the direction desired. Every organization manager and change agent — be it in business, government, volunteer organization, service organization, or home — has already developed some diagnostic schema. This presentation will look at a model of three interlocking internal systems that affect outputs. Hopefully it will help improve the quality of diagnosing and action taking. The table on page 88 shows that, according to this model, output variables are a result of three interlocking systems: the social system, the operation system, and the administrative system. Outputs are probably related in some degree to all three systems, but at a given time one system may be more responsible than the other. If such is the case, it is important that we try to take appropriate action in the dominant influencing system, or desired results probably will not occur. It should also be pointed out that the organization may be affected by external demand or client systems which need to be understood and managed.

System Diagnosis

This chapter focuses on those forces that function inside the organization. For diagnostic purposes it is a closed-system framework. All organizations are also open systems in the sense that they interact with the outside environment and both influence and are influenced by that environment. Such an open-system framework is presented in a later chapter.

Three Organizational Systems

The Social System

Every organization has its social world, that dynamic condition made up of people of different positions interacting with each other — talking, arguing, helping, deciding, solving problems — working in some way with each other, trying to achieve some of the goals of the organization and to satisfy some of their own personal needs. Every social system has some basic components:

1. *Climate.* The prevailing emotional state shared by members in the system, climate may be formal, relaxed, defensive, cautious, accepting, trusting.

2. *Communication network.* There are formal and informal patterns about who talks with whom, when, how often, and about what.

3. *Status-role structure.* There is always some division of labor, some people performing one function and others doing something else. Some persons have higher status than others, hence more power and usually more influence.

4. *Pattern of management.* Some people in the organization have the responsibility to work in superordinate positions relative to others, with the assignment to help subordinates in their work. The particular pattern or style of handling this superordinate action that develops in the social system starts at the top in an organization and tends to become the prevailing condition throughout (Likert, 1961).

5. *Decision-making method.* Since a basic process in any organization is to solve problems and make decisions, a method for handling problem-solving and decision-making requirements gets established in the social system. It is closely linked to the pattern of management but also includes whether decisions are made by few or many, the use of all relevant resources in problem solving, the creativity of decisions, and the degree of commitment to implement the decisions.

6. *Values and goals.* Organizations differ in that various social systems in the organization will identify certain factors as being more important than others and will place a higher value on them. Some of these valued items will become ends toward which effort is expended; they become the goals in the system. Social systems differ in terms of things valued and goals desired, how values and goals are established, and the degree to which members accept the values and goals and work toward them.

The Operation System

Every organization develops its method for getting work done — the unique arrangement of equipment, material, people, and processes used to accomplish work. A common industrial operation system is the assembly line, in which men are arranged along a conveyor belt of some type with the product to be assembled moving along the belt and each worker doing a specific task. The operation system can be altered by changing equipment, using different basic or raw materials, arranging people differently, or changing work assignments.

It is immediately apparent that the social system is integrally connected with the operation system, for the arrangements of people will affect their ability to communicate with each other. The work assignments and work flow will influence the pattern of management used and perhaps the ways decisions are made.

However, there are unique elements in the operation system distinct from the social system that can be altered separately, although some concomitant effects in the social system may be noticed. The operation system can be changed in any organization. A common university operation system shows a professor in a large lecture hall, standing at a podium in front, lecturing for a whole period. If the class is broken up into small student groups, arranged in a circle with the professor sitting in the circle, a different learning process is likely to occur. However, if the professor is still afflicted with his notions of status and his role as professor, he may continue to dominate the situation, to lecture, and to control the social system. For real change to take place, some modification is necessary in both the operation and social systems. But the professor in the lecture situation will probably find it almost impossible to change the basic nature of instruction unless some changes are made in the existing operation system.

The Administrative System

Interlacing the social and operation systems is a network of policy, procedure, auditing, and reporting that represents another whole system operating in connection with the other two but somewhat separate. Every organization has established certain formalized procedures for setting down the standards, rules, and regulations that influence what happens in the other two systems. Some important

Internal Systems That Influence Organization Outputs

Social System	+	Operation System	+	Administration System	=	Organization Output
•Climate •Status role •Decision making •Management style •Values •Communication •Goals		•Work flow •Equipment •Location •Physical environment •Material •Work arrangements •Schedules		•Policy •Wage-salary •Promotions •Fringe benefits •Hiring-firing •Raises •Budgets •Reporting •Auditing		•Profit/loss •Production •Costs •Absenteeism •Turnover •Commitment •Involvement •Apathy •Quality

elements in the administrative system are as follows:

1. *Wage and salary administration.* Organizations establish procedures by which pay levels are established and outline the ways in which increases in salary are obtained or bonuses or special benefits are possible.

2. *Hiring-firing-promotions.* Each organization has prescribed methods for hiring and firing and for making promotions — all laid out by the administrative system.

3. *Report-auditing.* Many organizations collect data on such matters as use of materials, finances, work output, and quality control. It usually takes the form of report-making or auditing procedures to help determine what is happening to resources.

4. *Fringe benefits.* More and more, organizations are establishing criteria and methods for allocating fringe benefits, such as leave time, vacations, sick leave, retirement, and insurance.

Organization Change by System Intervention

In the field of research on organizations, there are numerous examples of change attempts made (some successful and some not) by altering some aspect of one of these systems.

The Administrative System

Perhaps one of the most common and easiest ways to try to bring about changes occurs in the administrative system. The old Hawthorne studies describe attempts to change production by offering changes in the administrative system (Roethlisberger and Dickson, 1939). Workers in the bank wiring room were offered a bonus to produce over the existing level of production, but production remained constant despite the offer of a bonus — or even when the bonus was eliminated. The observer, gathering data from the workers, discovered that in the informal social system the workers agreed that if they increased production to get the bonus, either management would raise the base production level or management would see that fewer men could do the same amount of work and someone would be laid off. Since the existing situation was satisfactory to the workers, they agreed to maintain production at the existing level. It was also agreed that lower production brought tighter supervision; so a drop-off in production was not allowed. Informal sanctions were applied by the workers to each other when informal norms were violated. Thus an attempt to alter production by offering a bonus (a change in the administrative system) was not successful because of contrary conditions in the social system.

One management consultant described a situation where management in a production division became disturbed over obscene words written on the workers' rest room walls. It was agreed that this was a negative reflection on the company, and the strategy employed to eliminate this condition was to send a memo to the workers to the effect that this practice should stop immediately. New orders via memos are a common administrative method for inducing change. Evidently, the workers took the message as a challenge, and obscene words increased. Management warned the workers that punishments would follow, but the words continued. A whole series of strategy-counterstrategy moves then followed. A monitor was placed in the rest rooms to police the situation to no avail. Management was finally reduced to painting the walls every day at considerable expense and finally decided that the few obscene words they had at first were not worth all they were going through. All measures were stopped, and the number of words dropped down to the few there had been in the first place.

Most parents have tried the strategy of manipulating the administrative system as a means of inducing performance in children. In order to get children to study more, practice a musical instrument, clean up their room, or do their chores, parents will often offer greater rewards, such as larger allowances or more television, or will invoke penalties, such as no television or no allowance or no use of the car. This manipulation of the reward-punishment aspect of the administrative system in the home is reported by many parents as having limited positive effects.

The literature is replete with examples of experiments in altering the administrative system, trying to influence the organization outputs, with varying results. Manipulating wage and salary conditions is a common strategy (Rothe, 1960:20–27). One study, for example, showed that when girls in an English factory who were threading needles for other girls to use were put on a piece-rate system (a change in the administrative system in an attempt to reward people who worked harder) their production dropped from ninety-six dozen needles a day to seventy-five dozen a day. However, when they were told that when a girl reached a quota of 100 dozen per day, she could go home, production immediately jumped. On the average girls reached their quota 2½ hours early each day. Apparently, *money* incentives were not as important as *time* incentives for these girls, and an administrative change in wages was not as important as the time factor.

Apparently some improvements in organization outputs can be achieved by changing certain administrative practices, such as decreasing labor turnover by having better methods of personnel selection (Fleishman and Berniger, 1960: 63–69).

However, in reducing accidents on the job, a study in a large tractor factory showed that the factor most highly correlated with accidents was the degree of comfort in the shop environment. Men who had to work in physically uncomfortable environments were most likely to become involved in accidents. Thus attempts to reduce accidents by signs, awards, and threats apparently were not so effective as making some change in the operation system (Keenan, Kerr, and Sherman, 1951:89–91).

The Social System

Ross and Zander compared employees who terminated their work situation with those who stayed and found a major difference in the degree to which certain psychological needs were met. They state:

> In this study we establish the fact that the degree of satisfaction of certain personal needs supplied by a person's place of employment has a significant direct relationship to his continuing to work for that company. These personal needs are for recognition, for autonomy, for a feeling of doing work that is important, and for evaluation by fair standards. In addition, knowing important people in the organization is related to continued employment (Ross and Zander, 1957:27).

The fulfillment of these needs is a direct consequence of what goes on in the social system. People are recognized, evaluated, and given a feeling of doing worthwhile work in a context of working with others in the organization. Some changes in the operation system might affect autonomy, but changes in the administrative system without modification in the social system appear to have minimal effect. A great deal has been written about the effects of the pattern of management or supervision on organization outputs. This has been a major variable in research and is an important part of the social system. Supervision is related to productivity, but the relationship, though still important, is surprisingly low. Argyle and his associates conclude: "The differences in productivity in work groups resulting from contrasting methods of supervision were typically small, usually not larger than 15 percent of the total output" (Argyle, Gardner, and Ciofi, 1958).

The management pattern has also been found related to grievances and turnover (Fleishman and Harris, 1962). This indicates that, if one wishes to influence such organization outputs as productivity, turnover, and grievances, one factor located in the social system is the pattern of management.

Dubin, in summarizing the work on supervision and productivity, has this to say:

> There is no "one best" method of supervision. As in all human systems, there is variability in the systems of supervision of industrial and commercial work. Several styles of supervision are effective, but they are individually successful only in relation to appropriate work settings. Variety in supervisory behaviors may no longer be considered a challenge to choose the "one best" for all settings, but rather as a challenge to understand where each does or does not work (Dubin, 1965:47).

Dubin in his analysis clearly feels that the type of supervision is related to the type of operation system. He describes differing operation systems, such as unit production, mass production, and continuous production as operations that require alterations in management behavior.

In an extensive case analysis, Guest (1962) shows the effects on a manufacturing plant when the plant manager is changed. The new manager had a different style of management and introduced a number of changes in the social system, including regular report meetings where communications were opened to all supervisors in the plant. In addition, the new manager began to make a number of changes in the operation system by improving physical comfort in the working areas, relocating ovens in the paint department, changing the number and length of conveyor lines in the trim department, and replacing outmoded tools. As a result of these changes in both the social system and the operation (with supporting administrative changes), the output variables were also changed remarkably: labor costs were reduced 14 percent; from being highest in manufacturing costs, the plant was 15 percent lower in manufacturing costs than the next best performer; absenteeism dropped from 4.1 percent to 2.5 percent; and turnover dropped from 6.1 percent to 4.9 percent. In comparison to other plants, this one was a leader in quality, safety, indirect labor costs, and grievances (Guest, 1962:98–103).

Another case study by Marrow and others (Marrow, Bowers, and Seashore, 1967) describes the changes in output variables as a result of major changes in management pattern. In this case a company was acquired and changes introduced, especially in the social system. The resulting analysis showed that performance of operators was improved. Changes in the operation system were also made, and some in the administrative system. The authors conclude that the following changes were most important in the productivity of operators:

1. An earnings development program where individual counseling and help were given to individual operators
2. The weeding out of low earners
3. Training in interpersonal relations for supervisors and staff
4. Consultation and problem solving with groups of operators

The authors (1967:183) state:

> Although the technical changes ... were on a large scale and affected nearly every employee, we find from our analysis that these changes cannot be shown to have improved operator performance.

It would appear that items 1, 3, and 4 are changes in the social system, and item 2 — the weeding out of low earners — is a change in the administrative system, that is, a change in policy about low earners.

Likert (1967) describes a study of management in the sales division of a large organization. He found that all top sales units in the division were characterized by managers who had a high supportive style of management, high performance goals, and a well-organized sales plan. Managers in the low-producing sales units had low scores in both areas — supportive relations and performance goals. Likert feels that the presence of both these conditions is necessary in a manager's behavior:

> The preceding analysis shows that a manager who has high performance goals and excellent job organization but who relies solely on economic needs and direct pressure to motivate his men is very likely to be disappointed by their achievements. The noneconomic motives must be used fully, along with the economic needs, to create high performance goals and establish the level of motivational forces which yield high productivity (1967:64).

The Operation System

One of the strong exponents of the importance of the operation system in contributing to output variables has been Frederick Herzberg. He sees social and administrative system variables as essentially *hygiene* factors — factors which remove hazards from the environment but which are not real motivators toward greater achievement. For him the motivators are in the nature of the job itself, and any basic change in motivation and hence output must come in some change in the nature of the operation system. He says:

> Supervisory training in human relations is probably essential to the maintenance of good hygiene at work. This is particularly true for the many jobs, both at rank and file and managerial levels, in which modern industry offers little chance for the operation of the motivators. These jobs are atomized, cut and dried, monotonous. They offer little chance for responsibility and achievement and thus little opportunity for self-actualization. ... A man who finds his job challenging, exciting, and satisfying will perhaps tolerate a difficult supervisor (Herzberg, Mausner, and Snyderman, 1959).

System Conditions That Seem to Affect Output Variables

Social System	Operation System	Administrative System
•Workers are involved in setting goals and making decisions. •Communications are open, people are kept informed as to what is happening in the system. •High level of trust and acceptance exists. •Management is highly person-centered as well as concerned about production. •Management has high performance goals. •Workers feel needed, useful, doing something worthwhile. •Team spirit develops, and workers have pride in their work group. •Workers feel support, recognition from supervisors and others. •Workers experience "coaching" or help when needed. •No undue pressure is exerted.	•Physical conditions are comfortable — do not require excess work, and safety conditions prevail. •Operation system allows workers time to interact with each other and build social support. •Workers are responsible for the quality of output of the operation system. •Workers have some control over the operation system; they are not entirely controlled by it. •Operation system requirements are matched to an adequate degree to the personal resources of the workers. •Workers have an opportunity to use a variety of skills and abilities on the job, as desired. •Operation system does not require too many conflicting interfaces.	•Rules and regulations are jointly established by management and workers when feasible. •Policies and procedures do not restrict adequate development of the social system. •Formal rewards are given for appropriate management and worker behavior. •All benefits are distributed in an equitable fashion. •Procedures and rules are not inflexible, are amenable to modification. •Workers are involved in setting goals and doing work planning. •Restrictive reporting and auditing as control measures are not used. •Authority and responsibility are appropriately delegated. •Advancements and promotions result from open review between superior and subordinate.

Herzberg (1968) describes the marked change in output variables (increased productivity, lower turnover, and absenteeism) in a work situation where employees doing routine correspondence were allowed to enlarge the nature of their work. Work which had been done in a routine manner was modified to allow employees more control over their work and more responsibility for their own output. Such modifications that lead to increased responsibility, challenge, and opportunity for growth are the real motivators, according to Herzberg.

McGregor (1967) recognizes the importance of the operations system as it affects organization outputs. He discusses three different studies, all showing the effects on outputs of changing the basic operation of the work. In a coal mine in Britain, a textile mill in India, and an electronics firm in America, the basic operation system was changed from one in which the individual worker does a small specialized piece of the work to one in which each worker functioned in a team in producing the whole product. In each case, productivity increased up to 30 percent.

There is a difference between making a change in the basic work flow and making changes in physical conditions around the basic work operation. The Hawthorne studies began with an experiment looking at the effects of illumination on productivity. In agreement with the hypothesis, as lighting improved, production increased. However, much to the surprise of the experimenters, as lighting decreased, production reached an all-time high. It became apparent that in the social system the workers felt they should work harder because they were part of an experiment, and it was the motivation in the social system and not lighting that affected the output.

Later in the Hawthorne experiments, in the relay assembly test room, modifications were made in the operation system with the introduction of rest periods. Output increased markedly. However, in the last experimental conditions all rest periods were eliminated and production reached an all-time high. In analyzing the situation again, it appeared that production was more a function of building a close-knit social system than the alteration of the work with rest periods (Roethlisberger and Dickson, 1939).

Baveles and Strauss (Whyte, 1955:90–94) describe a situation in a toy factory where employees working in the paint section of an assembly line complained of the air circulation and asked for fans. Although engineers claimed that fans would not help, they were provided and production increased slightly. Then the employees asked to have the assembly line conveyor controlled by two speeds — fast and slower — and requested the right to regulate the belt to correspond with their physical reactions — to work hard when they felt fresh and slower when tired. This was also allowed and production improved sharply. However, the increased production from this section of the total assembly put pressures on workers on either side of the paint crew, who complained bitterly. Consequently, the management eliminated the modifications in the paint section. The foreman and many of the workers in the paint crew promptly resigned. This points out the necessity of seeing the interlocking nature of a total operation system and of being aware that change in one part may affect other parts of the system.

A classic study was done by Whyte in examining the restaurant industry. The existing work flow in certain restaurants showed that the operation system flowed from the waitress, who took the customer's order and passed the order directly to the cook, thus initiating work for him. Cooks often responded negatively to having lower-status waitresses initiating work for them and would often frustrate the waitress by slowing down her orders. When the work flow was altered by eliminating the contact between waitress and cook by means of a spindle or a barrier between them and when orders were passed in written form, tensions and disturbances decreased (Whyte, 1948).

Perhaps it would be possible to reduce tension and conflicts between waitresses and cooks by working at the social system level — giving them some human relations training and helping them accept each other and work more cooperatively together. However, the alteration of the operation system appears to be more easily accomplished.

Principle of System Reinforcement

An examination of the above framework and the supporting research evidence leads to the development of the following working principle: To maximize output variables, all three systems (social, operation, and administrative) should function in such a way that they are mutually reinforcing. The table on page 93 identifies the conditions that seem to be necessary in the three systems to support desired organization outputs.

A social system that develops pride in the work group, mutual support, interdependence between management and worker, and high trust and acceptance is essential. An operation system that keeps people isolated, working independently with no chance for interaction, and that has controls for quality required by others than the workers mediates against building the desired social system. If the above social system is desired, then an administrative system would *not* be supportive if it required checking up by supervisors, a tight audit and reporting procedure, secret reviews of performance, allocation of rewards determined by unilateral action by the person in charge, tight control of all expenditures authorized only by the top person, and delegation of authority only to assign work.

Likewise, it is extremely difficult to develop a creative and appropriate operation system or to revamp the administrative system if the social system is not functioning well. If in the social system management is oppressive and controlling, decisions are not shared, communications are closed, trust is low, and people are highly dependent or rebellious, then the ability to work out new, creative procedures and work systems will be drastically reduced.

Persons who are trying to influence output variables are often not aware of the interconnections in the systems. One company was trying to carry out a new policy of decentralization. As the company grew, it became important to give more authority and autonomy to plants in separate locations. Although the new policies gave more responsibility to the plant managers, top management for a number of unrecognized reasons did not allow managers control over capital expenditures. All expenditures over a few hundred dollars had to be cleared with the executive committee. Until this policy was changed, it was difficult to achieve the goals of decentralization.

One of the increasing trends in industry is toward automation. This is a major alteration of the operation system. Such a drastic modification of work operations of necessity will require appropriate changes in the social and administrative systems. Some analysis of these trends has already been done (Whyte, 1957; Walker, 1957).

Summary

It has been proposed here that organization outputs are a function of the effects of three interlocking internal systems — social, operation, and administrative. To alter the outputs seems to require some modification of all three systems; at least, a modification in one system should be supported by appropriate alterations in the others. It would appear that much of the current writing about organization development focuses primarily on changes in the social system. Likert writes about changing the organization from system 1 to system 4 (Likert, 1967) and is primarily concerned with changes in the social system. Analysis of social systems and strategies for change have come latest into the organization scene and have been given a great deal of needed attention. However, total organization development still requires both sound diagnosis of all systems that affect output and appropriate decisions for change based on the diagnosis.

References

Argyle, Michael, Godfrey Gardner, and Frank Ciofi
  1958 Supervisory methods related to productivity, absenteeism and labour turnover. *Human Relations* 11 (February): 24–25.

Dubin, Robert
  1965 *Leadership and Productivity.* San Francisco: Chandler Publishing Co.

Fleishman, Edwin A., and Joseph Berniger
1960   One way to reduce office turnover. *Personnel* 37 (May-June): 63–69.

Fleishman, Edwin A., and E. F. Harris
1962   Patterns of leadership behavior related to employee grievances and turnover. *Personnel Psychology* 15:43–56.

Guest, Robert H.
1962   *Organizational Change: The Effect of Successful Leadership.* Homewood, Ill.: Irwin-Dorsey Press.

Herzberg, Frederick
1968   Motivation, morale and money. *Psychology Today* 1 (March).

Herzberg, Frederick, B. Mausner, and B. Snyderman
1959   *The Motivation to Work.* New York: John Wiley and Sons.

Keenan, Vernon, Willard Kerr, and William Sherman
1951   Psychological climate and accidents in an automotive plant. *Journal of Applied Psychology* 35 (April): 89–91.

Likert, Rensis
1961   *New Patterns of Management.* New York: McGraw-Hill, Inc.

Likert, Rensis
1967   *The Human Organization.* New York: McGraw-Hill, Inc.

McGregor, Douglas
1967   *The Professional Manager.* New York: McGraw-Hill, Inc.

Marrow, A. J., D. E. Bowers, and S. E. Seashore
1967   *Management by Participation.* New York: Harper & Row Co.

Roethlisberger, Fritz J., and William J. Dickson
1939   *Management and the Worker.* Cambridge: Harvard University Press.

Ross, Ian C., and Alvin C. Zander
1957   Need satisfaction and employee turnover. *Personnel Psychology* 10 (Autumn): 327.

Rothe, Harold
1960   Does higher pay bring higher productivity? *Personnel* 37 (July-August): 20–27.

Walker, Charles R.
1957   *Toward the Automatic Factory.* New Haven: Yale University Press.

Whyte, William F.
1948   *Human Relations in the Restaurant Industry.* New York: McGraw-Hill, Inc.

Whyte, William F.
1955   *Money and Motivation.* New York: Harper & Row Co.

Whyte, William F.
1961   *Men at Work.* Homewood, Ill.: Irwin-Dorsey Press.

DIAGNOSIS FOR TEAM DEVELOPMENT

Modern society is a complex of organizations. Almost every facet of man's existence is serviced, regulated, assisted, or facilitated by one organization or another. The waking hours of almost every modern man are expended within the structures and processes of some type of organization — be it family, school, government, church, club, business, industry, or a combination.

An organization simply defined is the arrangement and utilization of resources (human, financial, and material) for the accomplishment of goals. Sometime in the life of almost every organization comes a point where its members are faced with two disturbing conditions that demand some pressure for change: One has to do with organizational consequences or outputs, and the other with organizational processes or dynamics. When either of these begins to falter, change considerations and strategies come into focus.

Organizational Outputs

All organizations, by definition, are goal oriented. When the goals — the ultimate output of the system — are not achieved in an adequate or satisfying degree, concern for change emerges. In our current economic system, all businesses are profit oriented. If the profit margin falls below a certain level defined as adequate, pressures for change will result. If profits are related to attendant conditions, such as production, sales, quality, products, service, labor turnover, or markets, some changes in these conditions need to be examined.

If the organization is service oriented — school, church, hospital, or government agency — and customer utilization of the service drops below the desired level, someone begins to plan for change. No organization can (or perhaps even should) continue to exist if it cannot maintain itself at some adequate level of organizational output or goal achievement. Pressures to make some change emerge with failing outputs, and it is generally the function of management to plan and take some action to minimize or reverse the output failures. A critical part of any manager's job has to do with planning an effective change strategy.

Organizational Processes

Within every organization there is also some standard of acceptable processes, dynamics, or means by which output is achieved. When conditions drop below this standard, whether it be formal or informal, managers begin to plan for change. Concern for change stems from two sources: (1) if processes drop too low, organizational outputs may be affected; and (2) if processes are too disrupted, the organization as a medium of human activity is too dissatisfying and the desire to improve the quality of life pushes for change, even though immediate outputs remain the same.

Almost no one enjoys working in a system where he is subjected to constant criticism, isolation, conflict, alienation, overcontrol, low need satisfaction, or feelings of futility and frustration. It is unlikely that any organization beset with these conditions could maintain its outputs over the long haul but, even disregarding the outputs, most modern managers would feel a responsibility for improving the general life quality of the human beings in the system.

If the standard of acceptable processes has been objectified, the organization can look at grievance rates, turnover rates, absenteeism, complaints, transfer requests, and early retirements as indicators that something in the organizational dynamics and processes is not functioning adequately, and again someone in management needs to begin to plan some changes. Even where objective criteria are not used, most managers are aware of certain climate factors, conflicts, or hostilities that are signs of process disruption — a signal that something needs to be done.

Change Strategies

Types of Strategies

In the long history of organizational life, numerous and varied strategies have become commonplace as measures that managers have adopted to induce change when output and process indicators have dropped below acceptable levels. Following is a partial list of such methods:

1. *Increased control.* In times of stress and crisis, especially

times when outputs are down, a very common method is to "get tough." This management strategy is characterized by "laying down the law," pushing employees harder, checking up more, expecting more work under consequence of penalty. This strategy does have its desired effects, at times, particularly over the short run.

2. *Cutbacks.* In order to show better profits, particularly results on paper, another method is to cut back on various resources — to lay off personnel, to eliminate certain programs or departments, to reduce inventories or budgets — and to expect the same or increased performance under these more austere conditions. This strategy is often accompanied by increased controls.

3. *Incentives.* If the diagnosis is that inadequate personnel performance is the cause of the low levels, one method for change is to offer inducements for higher performance — bonuses, incentive pay, profit sharing, promotions, or compensatory time. This is the reverse of increased control and operates from the assumption that personal benefit and financial rewards are major motivators for workers.

4. *Motivation devices.* Managers may try to solve problems by thinking up a new wrinkle, twist, or device that will stimulate new or better performance. Such activities are contests of various kinds, interdepartmental competitions, slogans, propaganda campaigns, special awards and recognitions, guest lecturers, or visits from "authorities."

5. *Consultants.* Starting with Jethro's visit to Moses (Exodus, chapter 18), the management and organization consultant has been a familiar organization figure. The hope is that an outside expert can come into the situation, see quickly what is wrong, and in one master stroke (or even a series of less masterly strokes) come up with a solution to the existing problem conditions.

Effectiveness of Strategies

Use of the above devices has had mixed results through the years. At times cutbacks have been beneficial and have produced good results. At other times the cutbacks have shown paper profits in the short run, but over a longer time span have proven disastrous for the effective functioning of the organization. Such mixed results are true for each of these strategies. The effectiveness of a strategy is a result of the following:

1. *Adequate diagnosis.* If the strategy employed is based on a sound diagnosis of the organizational situation, it has the possibility of producing a positive result. However, if the strategy is employed out of the personal desire, need, or inclination of some person or persons at the top and is not really related to the basic condition in the system, reversal effects may occur.

2. Creative problem solving. Even if the diagnosis is correct, the "right" solution is not always evident. It is one thing to find out that low employee morale is the cause for poor production. It is quite another to devise an effective solution to the problem, one that is based on adequate data, is reality tested, affords new and innovative processes or thrusts, and is feasible in terms of the constraints of time and resources.

3. Commitment. Any new strategy has a greater probability for achieving the desired impact if it has the support of those who must implement it — if they are committed to expending their time and energies to achieve the new goals. Lack of commitment may indeed be one of the basic problems, and the improved strategy may try to induce that commitment by threats, rewards, or motivation "devices." But the commitment to change is an important element in producing increased performance.

Team Building: A Method of Revitalizing an Organization

When a unit that is composed of human beings arranged together to reach goals finds that it no longer has the capability to solve its problems well or reach its goals at an acceptable level, it may need to look for a way to reshape itself.

Team building is the current designation given to a process for revitalizing a system. Human systems have a tendency to become established, routinized, and institutionalized around certain procedures, methods, and processes that may not really be functional given the current demands. A number of writers have described in various ways the different kinds of human systems currently found in organizations. McGregor (1960) first alluded to them when he talked about Theory X and Y as alternative assumptions of management. A Theory-X manager assumes that people are basically lazy and unconcerned about work and the organization, that they must be pushed and regulated if work is going to be accomplished. Conversely, a Theory-Y manager sees people as fundamentally industrious, wanting to work, concerned about the organization, and able to make a useful contribution. The terms have been commonly transposed into regarding a Theory-X organization or system as one with rigid management, high control by authority, and minimal use of its human resources. Similar orientations have been described by Likert (1967), Blake and Mouton (1964), Argyris (1964), and others.

The Likert model describes four types of systems, ranging from authoritarian to participative. Blake and Mouton use their grid to categorize organizations from 1-1 (minimal concern about people and production) to 9-9 (maximum concern about people and production). Argyris uses Maslow's hierarchy of needs to look both at organizations that concentrate on man's lower needs (for safety and biological comfort) and those that encourage the total development of the people in the system. He points out that many organizations function to keep people at a low level of effectiveness but could be organized and managed to release human potential.

If an organization is diagnosed as being a restrictive, authoritarian system with resulting inadequate outputs or dysfunctional processes, how does a manager change it to one that is more productive and effective? This is what team building may make possible.

Goals in Team Building

Using the orientations named above, the overall goal of team building is to develop a social system that exhibits the characteristics of a highly effective, people-building, potential-releasing, goal-achieving organization. Some elements of that kind of system are these:

1. *Climate of high social support.* Likert (1961) describes social support this way:

> The leadership and other processes of the organization must be such as to ensure a maximum probability that in all interactions and in all relationships within the organization, each member, in the light of his background, values, desires, and expectations, will view the experience as supportive and one which builds and maintains his sense of personal worth and importance.

Others have talked about a climate where there are high trust among members, feelings of concern, fulfillment of a personal need for social interaction and self-esteem.

2. *Open communication process.* The goal in open communication is to achieve the capability and the method for making all relevant data available to the decision makers.

3. *Creative problem solving.* As indicated earlier, the organization should be able to make an adequate diagnosis of its own problems and then innovate creative solutions to these problems.

4. *Commitment.* Following the making of decisions, an important factor is high commitment on the part of members to support and implement the decisions made.

5. *Achievement of individual and organizational goals.* The system must achieve that neat balance between helping individuals meet important personal needs and at the same time reaching organizational goals that allow for the continuation of the organization at an appropriate level. Organizations must be goal oriented — that is the reason for their existence. Personnel in the organization must help achieve the goals, but a great deal of current research indicates that people are not willing to sacrifice themselves on the altar of the organization.

6. *Interdependence and team effort.* In an effective unit there is a meshing of resources as people combine their efforts to achieve

goals. Interdependence is a state in which each person functions at a high level of utilization of his own resources as he uses the resources of others. The opposite of interdependence is dependency or counter-dependency. In a dependency situation the authority person dominates, and others are passive responders to authority demands. Counterdependency represents resistant or rebellious reactions against authority. Independence connotes a condition of separateness in which people go their own ways rather than working in connection with each other.

Team effort is the result of high interdependency. This does not mean "management by committee" in the sense that no one is responsible. In a good team each player has his assignment and feels responsible for its achievement but tries to combine his efforts with the efforts of others with a resulting synergistic effect, as the whole is greater than the sum of its independent parts.

A Team-development Program

When signals indicate that the working unit is not functioning effectively (work is late, assignments are missed, conflicts are apparent, people are not supporting each other), it is time for the manager to think about conducting a team-building session. One must periodically stop a machine and see that it gets appropriate overhaul and maintenance. So it is with human machinery, particularly a human group.

103

Team-development programs have been conducted with a variety of designs and formats, but one simple, useful way of conducting a team-building program is the following:

1. Take at least one day off for the team-building effort and get away from the work site so there will not be any interruptions.

2. Ask each person to write his answers to the following questions and be prepared to share them with others at the meeting:

    a. What keeps you from being as effective as you would like to be in your position?

    b. What keeps the staff (unit or department) from functioning as an effective team?

    c. What do you like about this unit that you want to maintain?

    d. What suggestions do you have for improving the quality of our working relationships and the functioning of our department?

3. At the meeting have each person read or present his responses to the above questions as a recorder writes them all on a blackboard or flipchart. There will then be four lists: (1) blocks to individual effectiveness, (2) blocks to team effectiveness, (3) things people like, and (4) suggestions for improvement.

4. Let the group then list according to priority the problems on which they want to work. These form the agenda for the meeting.

5. Permit the group to begin work on achieving the goal of the team-development session, to eliminate as many obstacles as possible. This may include changing assignments, clarifying roles, clearing up misunderstandings, giving more information, or making other innovations. The important thing is to start the team in a process of regularly looking at its own effectiveness and working on solutions to its own problems.

Team building is a relatively new program for increasing the effectiveness of working units. A program for looking at work relationships with the goal of working out clearer arrangements, better communications, greater coordination, and better decisions is a sensitive process. The manager who moves in this direction should prepare well; he may even need some outside resource person to help in the firs. program. But with careful planning, commitment from unit members, and a certain willingness to risk, team building can pay big dividends.

References

Argyris, Chris
  1964 *Integrating the Individual and the Organization.* New York: John Wiley & Son.

Blake, Robert R., and Jane S. Mouton
  1964 *The Managerial Grid.* Houston: Gulf Publishing Co.

Likert, Rensis
    1961   *New Patterns of Management.* New York: McGraw-Hill.

Likert, Rensis
    1967   *The Human Organization.* New York: McGraw-Hill.

McGregor, Douglas
    1960   *The Human Side of Enterprise.* New York: McGraw-Hill.

DISPARITY, MOTIVATION, AND PLANNING FOR CHANGE*

Almost all change results from someone's deciding to bring about alterations, either personally or as a director of changes in organization structure or operations. Institutions and organizations change in part as human personalities act upon them, and so one common strategy for producing organization change is to try to create a desire in an individual in an organization to engage in a change program.

Most management-training programs, and especially those that are laboratory-based, start with this change premise: If the manager at the program can be "motivated" to want to begin engaging in new behaviors, this is the beginning of the whole change-development sequence.

Disparity Models

Most of the popular theories or models about managerial behavior have a disparity condition built into their formulations. All disparity models are based on the assumption that a change strategy must create a recognition of the difference between what an individual holds as his goal, objective, or ideal and what he is actually doing, thinking, or accomplishing. When a model presents an "ideal" state or style of management which either explicitly or implicitly is held up as the goal a manager should achieve, persons perceiving the model cannot help but compare their own real state with the ideal, and if it is perceived as being less than the ideal, a disparity condition has been created which will push toward improvement

---

*With Philip B. Daniels.

Minimum and Maximum Positions in Current Management Theories

Theorist	Minimum Position	Maximum Position
Douglas McGregor	Theory X: Assumptions that managers hold about people: they dislike work, need coercion, want security, want direction.	Theory Y: Assumption of manager that worker likes work, is self-motivated, accepts responsibility.
Rensis Likert	System 1: Exploitive, authoritative management. High control of people by the manager.	System 4: Participative group. Manager allows worker to participate in organizational matters with him.
Robert Blake and Jane Mouton	1-1 Style: Low concern for both production or results and people.	9-9 Style: Optimum concern for both production, goals, results, and the people who must achieve the results.
Abraham Maslow	Management concerned with only physiological or safety needs.	Eupsychian management: Self-actualized managers dealing with self-actualized people.

in performance. A number of current management theories are reviewed in the table of minimal and maximal conditions. Presumably, all managers fall somewhere between the high (ideal) and low types.

Management-development programs that use one or more of the above theories as a base usually attempt, by a variety of methods, to get managers to see themselves at some point between the low and the high positions and then to plan some type of change to try to move closer to the ideal level.

How to Create Awareness of Disparity

There are currently a variety of methods used to create an awareness of the disparity between existing and ideal conditions:

1. Cognitive Insight

Most literature, lectures, and training films that use a disparity theory try to get the reader, hearer, or viewer to engage in personal analysis. It is hoped that the manager, through his own internal dialogue, will have some insight about himself and will see himself somewhere below the ideal. It is obvious that merely presenting information in any form, without some external factors present, cannot ensure that the respondent will see himself accurately.

2. Interpersonal Feedback

A second method is to create an opportunity for a manager to get direct, immediate, and hopefully accurate and helpful feedback about his management style from people who have interacted with him. The open exchange of verbal feedback, which allows the manager an opportunity to ask questions and push for detail as he checks with others, is seen by many as the most personal disparity model and the one with the most impact. The assumption is that either the person receiving the feedback is unaware of his impact on others, or his self-perception is at odds with reality. In either case the feedback should reveal enough disparity to move him toward change.

3. Surveys or Instruments

There are a number of data-gathering instruments that help a person get extensive and sometimes statistically precise data about his own performance, style, and impact. These instruments are circulated to people who work with the manager, they are then tabulated and summarized, and the data is fed back to the manager. Again there is the assumption that the data will reveal a disparity and bring about change.

Problems in Using Disparity Models

There are a number of issues that plague all disparity models, particularly those emphasizing feedback as the method of producing disparity. The more important issues are these:

1. Who Reveals the Disparity?

Without feedback it is difficult to see where one is in comparison with the ideal. If a person feels he would like to be at System 4 (participative management), from whom does he need feedback to get a clear picture of his actual performance? Who are the important reference persons whose feedback will make a difference? One can imagine a manager getting feedback from subordinates or peers he does not respect and immediately discounting the data. Or one could get feedback from one's boss and be so responsive to that important figure that all change is based on that one piece of data, with complete disregard for other sources of information.

2. How Intense Is the Feedback?

Do people respond more to high-intensity feedback, where issues are strongly stated and the emotional loading is great; or do people hear feedback better if the information comes "low key," in a more gentle or restrained manner? Do some people with their own unique personality characteristics respond to high-intensity feedback and others to low-key responses? If so, how do we determine who is to receive what kinds of data? Or do we disregard this factor and give all people the same information?

3. How Much Data Should Be Given?

If we are going to maximize the possibility that a person will change some aspects of his behavior, is it better to give him one piece of information at a time so that he does not feel overwhelmed? Or is it better to unload all the data so that he can have a total picture of his performance and, starting with this "gestalt," do a better job of planning? Are people overwhelmed with too much feedback, or do they simply shrug off sketchy data?

4. How Is the Disparity Revealed?

Is it better to create disparity by having a one-shot feedback session, or would a series of sessions be better? Is it best done on the job in the work setting or away from the job in a setting more relaxed and conducive to introspection and reflection? Is it best done by personal one-to-one feedback or through an instrumented process where data-gathering devises are used and one can review the data in private?

5. When Should Disparity Be Revealed?

Do you get more impact from feedback if it is given when a person asks for it or when someone wants to share it? Does it come best immediately after an interaction or exchange or later when people have had a chance to think things over? Does feedback early in one's job life have more impact than after one has been entrenched in his position for years? What happens if the disparity is created at a time when a person is being reviewed for a raise in salary or a promotion? Timing must be an important factor.

Using feedback as a method of creating disparity must be managed carefully and the above issues well considered. It is possible that a person may be given so much feedback by threatening power people, in such an intense way, that the resulting disparity overwhelms him and leads to his leaving the situation or giving up in despair. The feedback has not then had the motivational results desired.

Goal Setting and Planning as a Disparity-reducing Process

Another method of reducing one's disparity level and changing to a more ideal state is goal setting. All management-by-objectives (MBO) programs are based on this method. If a person sees by any method that where he is is not where he would like to be, he then can set goals that represent the ideal state to be achieved. The disparity

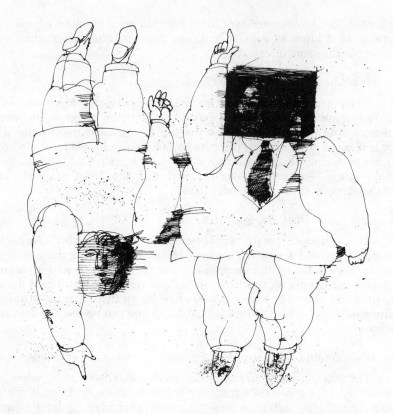

is the gap between his current level and the new goal. Disparity is reduced as the person who has a commitment to the goal can actually move his performance closer to his desired state.

An important part of this disparity-reducing process is good planning. After a person has identified a goal (such as "I want to be a more effective manager"), he needs to engage in specific planning centered around working through specific subgoals. The action steps are as follows:

1. Specify Clearly Stated Subgoals

An effective plan is generally designed to attain specific, clearly stated subgoals, which, combined, will help achieve the overall goal. For example: a subgoal "to hold an effective staff meeting every Monday and review all plans and decisions" would help a person reach his major goal, which is to become a more effective manager.

2. Specify Clearly Stated Action Steps

Since a plan is basically a description of actions that someone will take at some time in the future, it is essential that the description be specific and clearly stated. If it is composed of general resolutions, the likelihood that the plan will be useful is relatively low. If it specifies what will be done, where it will be done, with whom it will be done, and so on, the plan has a much better chance of succeeding.

3. State Definite Time-frame

Among the specifics in the plan should be the time-frame. The manager should make it clear exactly when he will begin his program of change, when his various specific actions will occur, and when he will evaluate his progress. In the meeting example, the plan would state that staff meetings would start next Monday, everyone would be informed a week in advance, an agenda would be distributed, and time would be allowed for discussion and a critique of the meeting.

4. Identify Social Supports

One of the most important principles having to do with planning personal change pertains to the involvement of other people in the change process. It is highly recommended that the manager plan to negotiate with other people in his work situation a kind of informal contract that will help him implement his plan. For example, he should commit himself publicly to his change goals, share with others his plans, appeal for their help, and get them to commit themselves to do specific things that will help implement the plan. In the past we have found that the manager's secretary is often a very able support person. Peers and colleagues may also be helpful. Some most dramatic effects have resulted when a manager used his boss as a support person. He should also be encouraged to consider sharing his plan with his subordinates and to involve them in the process of helping him change and develop. Since his plan is very likely to involve changing the way he relates to them, having their support is essential.

5. Specify Sources of Reinforcement

Generally speaking, managers are able to change their style of managing others when their new behavior produces positive results. Anytime a person begins experimenting with new behavior, he runs the risk that it will not be effective. Insofar as he can in the planning phase, the manager should plan to do things that have at least a fair chance of succeeding. Managers sometimes find it difficult to build into their plans provisions for their own reinforcement, but if they are able to do so, their chances for success are likely to increase. Giving people praise and recognition for contributions at the staff meeting should reinforce the goal of holding better meetings.

111

6. *Make Provision for Evaluation*

Closely related to the reinforcement issue is the need for on-going evaluation. The manager will, no doubt, be eager to know how he is doing as he implements his plan. He will be able to get some indication from the visible effects he has on others and from the consequences his behavior has on his general level of productivity as it is usually assessed. However, it is very desirable for him to build into his plan the specific action steps he will take at some point in time to receive feedback on specific elements in his change plan.

One approach to evaluation is for the manager to schedule open feedback sessions with people who have been in a position to see how he has been doing during the period of implementation. They may be the "social support" people with whom he will have been working. He could hold one-to-one sessions with individuals, or he could meet with a group, such as a staff or collection of key people, who could help him evaluate his new effectiveness.

7. *Write Out the Plan*

Not only the subgoals the manager develops out of the feedback, but also the plans he makes in order to attain those subgoals, should be written down in detail. He should be encouraged not to file his plan away, but to keep it readily available so he can refer to it periodically as he attempts to do the specific things he has outlined for himself. In four to six months, when he attempts to evaluate the effectiveness of his efforts to change, it will be very useful for him to take out his written plan and use it as part of the evaluation process. If he fails to write down his plan in detail, the likelihood that he will implement it is significantly reduced.

Goal setting and effective planning are important methods for bringing about needed changes. Disparity may provide the motivation, but planning and action produce results.

References

Blake, Robert R., and Jane S. Mouton
   1964   *The Managerial Grid.* Houston: Gulf Publishing Co.

Dalton, Gene, and Paul Lawrence
   1971   *Motivation and Control in Organizations.* Homewood, Ill.: Irwin-Dorsey.

Likert, Rensis
   1967   *The Human Organization.* New York: McGraw-Hill.

Maslow, Abraham
   1965   *Eupsychian Management.* Homewood, Ill.: Irwin-Dorsey.

McGregor, Douglas
   1960   *The Human Side of Enterprise.* New York: McGraw-Hill.

CREATIVITY IN ORGANIZATIONS*

Creativity has been given a great deal of attention over the past twenty years. Most research, however, has been centered on identifying forces within an individual related to his creative output and endeavor, on discovering factors akin to creativity, and on looking at ways to measure creativity in individuals. Less has been done in investigating organizational conditions that tend to foster and release creative behavior in employees, and even less attention has been paid to the management process. No one has adequately answered such questions as, "How do you go about managing people in a way that either releases or inhibits their creative efforts?" In fact, the whole process of changing conditions in organizations to facilitate creative output has not been dealt with to any great extent.

Creativity and Organization Development

For profit-making organizations, the problem regarding creativity has to do with solid profit and loss, for such companies are concerned with producing new products or services in order to compete in the marketplace. To meet the need for a consistent flow of new products, many organizations have established, in recent years, research and development units with the special function of generating new product ideas. Management of the research and development unit however, is just now coming under investigation. Important

---

*In collaboration with Randall R. Scott.

113

questions are these: Does a manager of an R & D unit manage in the same way as he would if he were managing a sales, manufacturing, marketing, or financial unit? To what extent do different kinds of activities require different management styles and orientations? Do creative persons require new and different styles and behaviors in their superiors?

In addition to the R & D solution of meeting the need for creative products or services, almost all organizations find themselves faced with a whole range of decisions and actions that would benefit from more imagination and creativity. For example, most business organizations could benefit from imagination in developing new markets, new sales methods, new uses of equipment, and in discovering new solutions to personnel and administrative problems.

Probably almost all areas of any organization could profit from some type of action that would develop more creative solutions to problems. This fact introduces one of the major current dilemmas in the organization development (O.D.) field: It is highly possible that current O.D. efforts may be antithetical to the release of creativity in organizations. Most O.D. activity begins with engaging in extensive team building within each working unit. The emphasis in team building centers in developing a climate of trust and openness in which people can begin to relate more authentically with each other, where a sense of cohesion and identity can be fostered in the work unit. Often team building will include such things as decision making by consensus and achieving interdependence in the work unit so that people work and support each other in effective team effort.

Although team development may be vitally needed in some organizations, is it needed in every one? A legitimate question is raised: If we emphasize collaboration, consensus decision making, cohesion, interdependence, and building work units where people's social needs for inclusion, warmth, and connectedness are met, to what extent do we inhibit organizational creativity? Perhaps too little attention has been given some of the side effects of current O.D. developments.

The Creative Individual

As the literature on creativity is examined, evidence is ample that the highly creative person is a nonconformist in many ways. (See research summary of characteristics of the creative individual.)

How much would current O.D. efforts, which place emphasis on integration and to some extent on conformity and cohesion, restrict and inhibit the highly individualistic, somewhat unorthodox, creative person? If we maximize the importance of the cohesive work unit, do we at the same time reduce the creative process that might unleash innovative potential in work unit members?

Research Summary of Characteristics of the Creative Individual*

I. Traits seen in perceptual habits
  A. Tolerance of ambiguity (can live with areas of confusion)
    1. Preference for complexity in phenomena
    2. Preference for imbalance in phenomena
    3. Openness to variety in phenomena
  B. Breadth of interest
  C. Perceptual control
    1. Flexibility
    2. Deferment of judgment
II. Traits seen in awareness of self
  A. Personal complexity
  B. Rejection of suppression as a means of controlling impulse
  C. Immediacy of response to stimuli
III. Traits seen in interaction with others
  A. Self-assertion; tendency to dominate through drive
  B. Verbal fluency
  C. Impulsiveness
  D. Expansiveness
  E. Noncomformity
  F. Tendency to release tension readily through motor activity
  G. Independence of judgment
IV. Traits seen in motivation
  A. Rapid personal tempo
  B. High level of drive
V. Traits in relation to others
  A. Not a joiner, has few close friends
  B. Relatively little interest in interpersonal relations
  C. Independence from parents
VI. Traits in job attitudes
  A. Preference for things and ideas to people
  B. High regard for intellectual interests
  C. Less emphasis on and value in job security
  D. Less enjoyment in and satisfaction from detail work and routine
  E. High level of resourcefulness and adaptability
  F. Scepticism
  G. Precision and critical ability; honesty
  H. Persistence
VII. Other traits
  A. Spontaneity
  B. Stubbornness
  C. Adventurousness
  D. Anxiety

Creative Organizations and Management

Very little hard research has looked at conditions characteristic of highly creative organizations. It is difficult to identify an organization or a specific unit in an organization that would be generally accepted as consistently creative. However, some thinking has been done in this area, as indicated by the table comparing the creative

---

*Adapted from Barron (1969).

Comparison of the Creative Individual
and the Creative Organization*

The Creative Individual	The Creative Organization
A. Conceptual fluency; is able to produce a large number of ideas quickly	A. Has idea men, open channels of communication, and ad hoc devices, such as suggestion systems, brainstorming, and idea units absolved of other responsibilities; encourages contact with outside sources
B. Originality; generates unusual ideas	B. Heterogenous personnel policy; includes marginal, unusual types; assigns nonspecialists to problems; allows eccentricity
C. Separates source from content in evaluating information; is motivated by interest in problem; follows wherever it leads	C. Has an objective, fact-founded approach; ideas evaluated on their merits, not on status of originator; has ad hoc approaches, such as anonymous communications and blind votes; selects and promotes on merit only
D. Suspends judgment; avoids early commitment; spends more time in analysis, exploration	D. Lack of financial, material commitment to products, policies; invests in basic research; uses flexible, long-range planning; experiments with new ideas rather than prejudging on "rational" grounds; everything gets a chance
E. Less authoritarian; has relativistic view of life	E. More decentralized, diversified; administrative slack, time and resources to absorb errors; risk-taking ethos; tolerates and expects taking chances
F. Accepts own impulses; playful, undisciplined exploration	F. Not run as "tight ship"; employees have fun; allows freedom to choose and pursue problems and freedom to discuss ideas
G. Independence of judgment, less conformity	G. Organizationally autonomous
H. Deviant, sees self as different	H. Original and different objectives, not trying to be another "X"
I. Rich, "bizarre" fantasy life and superior reality orientation; controls	I. Security of routine; allows innovation; "Philistines" provide stable, secure environment that allows "creators" to roam

*Adapted from Steiner (1965).

116

individual and the creative organization. This table shows that certain conditions in the current O.D. framework are also present in the creative organization. However, there are some additional conditions in the creative organization that, up to now at least, have not been generally thought of as an important part of an O.D. effort. For example, the creative organization encourages marginal and unusual types of people. It allows eccentricity. It has a range of unique ad hoc devices which would encourage free thinking and new ideas. It sets up norms for risk taking and tolerates the new and the unexpected. It emphasizes a fun-loving atmosphere with freedom to pursue ideas not in the main stream of the organization. And it encourages the different and the bizarre and offers freedom to roam and to engage in pursuits not ordinarily part of organizational routine.

If these are characteristics of creative organizations, how do we begin to train managers to create these conditions rather than conditions that seem at present to pay off more in the organizational system? Most managers are rewarded if they can create a smooth-working, functioning unit that operates efficiently and effectively. The highly creative unit in an organization might not be seen as smooth-working and efficient. It might appear jagged and uneven and rather kooky or crazy to an outside or inside observer. Can an organization tolerate that? Can we train and reward managers who can produce conditions outside the mainstream of current organizational thinking?

117

Encouragement of Creativity through Management and Organization*

This scale will help you see to what extent the type of management and the organizational conditions support and encourage creative effort.

Conditions Discouraging Creativity		Conditions Encouraging Creativity
1. My ideas or suggestions never get a fair hearing.	1 2 3 4 5 6 7	My ideas or suggestions get a fair hearing.
2. I feel that my boss is not interested in my ideas.	1 2 3 4 5 6 7	I feel that my boss is very much interested in my ideas.
3. I receive no encouragement to innovate on my job.	1 2 3 4 5 6 7	I am encouraged to innovate on my job.
4. There is no reward for innovating or improving things on my job.	1 2 3 4 5 6 7	I am rewarded for innovating and improving on my job.
5. There is no encouragement for diverse opinions among subordinates.	1 2 3 4 5 6 7	There is encouragement of diversity of opinion among subordinates.
6. I'm very reluctant to tell my boss about mistakes I make.	1 2 3 4 5 6 7	I feel comfortable enough with my boss to tell him about mistakes I make.
7. I'm not given enough responsibility for me to do my job right.	1 2 3 4 5 6 7	I am given enough responsibility for me to do my job right.
8. To really succeed in this organization, one needs to be a friend or a relative of the boss.	1 2 3 4 5 6 7	There is no favoritism in the organization.
9. There are other jobs in this organization that I would prefer to have.	1 2 3 4 5 6 7	I have the job in this organization that I think I do best.
10. They keep close watch over me too much of the time.	1 2 3 4 5 6 7	They trust me to do my job without always checking on me.
11. They would not let me try other jobs in the organization.	1 2 3 4 5 6 7	I could try other kinds of jobs in the organization if I wanted to.
12. The management is made very uptight by confusion, disorder, and chaos.	1 2 3 4 5 6 7	The management deals easily with confusion, disorder, and chaos.
13. There is a low standard of excellence on the job.	1 2 3 4 5 6 7	There is a high standard of excellence for me on the job.

*With Philip B. Daniels.

118

14. My boss is not open to receive my opinion about how he might improve his own performance on the job.　1 2 3 4 5 6 7　My boss is very open to suggestions on how he might improve his own performance.

15. My boss has a very low standard for judging his own performance.　1 2 3 4 5 6 7　My boss has a very high standard of excellence for judging his own performance.

16. I am not asked for suggestions on how to improve service to the customers.　1 2 3 4 5 6 7　The management actively solicits my suggestions and ideas on how to improve the service to customers.

17. My boss shows no enthusiasm for the work in which we are engaged.　1 2 3 4 5 6 7　My boss exhibits lots of enthusiasm for the work in which we are engaged.

18. Mistakes get you in trouble; they aren't to learn from.　1 2 3 4 5 6 7　Around here mistakes are to learn from and not to penalize you.

19. Someone else dictates how much I should accomplish on my job.　1 2 3 4 5 6 7　I'm allowed to set my own goals for my job.

20. I am very much dissatisfied with my job.　1 2 3 4 5 6 7　I am very much satisfied with my job.

21. My boss never lets me know how I stand with him.　1 2 3 4 5 6 7　My boss keeps me informed on how I stand with him.

22. My boss does not communicate clearly what I am to do.　1 2 3 4 5 6 7　My boss communicates clearly what I am supposed to do.

23. The organization has too many rules and regulations for me.　1 2 3 4 5 6 7　The organization has adequate rules and regulations for me.

The table "Encouragement of Creativity through Management and Organization" identifies some management and organization conditions that release or inhibit people's creative actions. By completing the scale, it may be possible to begin to identify the areas where change may be needed.

One research study of organizational situations identified favorable and unfavorable conditions for creativity. Taylor, Smith, and Ghiselin (reporting on research interviews conducted among scientists at the personnel laboratory, Air Force Systems Command, Lackland Air Force Base, Texas) summarized thirteen conditions felt by the scientists to be unfavorable and five conditions felt to be favorable for creative and productive work in science. The unfavorable conditions mentioned most frequently were instability of the budget, conflict between the demands of management activities and research activities, inadequacies in supportive groups and procedures, inadequacies in compensation and other attractions, lack of professional internship for young scientists, poor communications with scientists working elsewhere on related problems, inadequacy of physical facilities, dearth of suitable recognition, exclusion of scientists from high-level decision making on scientific problems, insufficient long-range planning in the total scientific program, interference between contract monitoring and regular research activities, inefficiency in selection and placement programs, and lack of personal counseling for scientists. The five conditions felt to be favorable were certain individual freedoms, intellectual challenges of the work, location and certain facilities, relative stability of the employment, and encouragement of continual training. These are some of the conditions that persons interested in improving creativity in organizations should examine carefully.

Training for Organizational Creativity

Does a person who has the ability to produce creative ideas also become an effective manager? Should we look for a creative manager in a creative person, or do we look for a manager who has the ability to manage creative people although he himself may not be particularly creative? When we examine current management-training methods, it is dubious that there is a great deal of emphasis or reward given to the highly individualistic, nonconforming, creative person. Very little emphasis has been placed on developing the ability to guide and stimulate the creative efforts of others. In a typical management-development program with an experience-based focus, a common occurrence is to see the nonconformist, the rebel, the individualistically oriented person with deviant behaviors and peculiar idiosyncracies as the object of initial negative reactions and negative feedback. It appears that a person would learn in this kind of training experience that the way to get along best with others is to conform to their expectations. If he can identify the group norms and can modify his behavior to fit in adequately to those norms, he will experience the warmth, acceptance, and rewards of the group. Perhaps these are not the conditions that should be emphasized in training if we are to encourage the creative person or if we are to train managers to work effectively with creative people or to release the creative potential of others. Perhaps the current training mode is not the most appropriate way of proceeding. It is also possible, however, to create a training process that emphasizes a set of norms entirely different from the ones mentioned above. Here, using the same methodology, a whole new set of behaviors could be identified and encouraged in management-development programs.

The Need for Innovation

As I have worked in organizations, my diagnosis of some systems is that what they need is not more trust, increased collaboration, better relationships, or even greater effort. They are hard-working units, doing a good job, and working quite well together. The major deficiency, as I see it, is that the people and their programs are in a rut. They keep doing the same things the same way even though conditions and problems change. For some reason new ideas, new solutions to problems, new services, new organization forms, procedures, or processes are not really encouraged or fostered. If such an organization were to improve its effectiveness, it would be the result of an effort to stimulate greater innovation — find more interesting, stimulating, and effective ways to function, solve problems, render services, or improve the product. This would require a form of organization development quite different from a development program for an organization bogged down in conflict, rivalry, suspicion, and low trust.

Management Actions That Foster Creativity

Steiner (1965) has identified five management behaviors that encourage the development of creativity:

1. *Values and rewards.* The creative organization prizes and rewards creativity. A management philosophy that stresses creativity as an organizational goal, that encourages and expects it at all levels, will increase the chances of its occurrence.

2. *Compensation.* It is probably this simple: Where creativity and not productivity is in fact the goal, then creativity and not productivity should in fact be measured and rewarded.

3. *Channels for advancement.* To the extent possible, there should be formal channels for advancement and status within the area of creativity.

4. *Freedom.* Within rather broad limits, creativity is increased by giving creators freedom in choice of problem and method of pursuit.

5. *Communication.* Many observations point to the importance of free and open channels of communication, both vertical and horizontal.

Elements of a Development Program in Creativity

1. *Assessment.* Using an instrument similar to the one in the table "Encouragement of Creativity through Management and Organization," the organization could be analyzed as to its current level of innovation and the employees' desire or need for more creative effort in their work.

2. *Action planning.* Based on the assessment, a plan of action for stimulating innovation could be developed. Depending on the assessment, some of the following actions might be taken:

a. Have seminars on creative thinking.

121

b. Have a reward-bonus incentive program for new, productive ideas.

c. Give people some free time for individual, or group, creative problem solving.

d. Devise a new kind of staff meeting that will let people free-wheel, brainstorm, or come up with new ideas easily.

e. Form new or unusual short-term groupings to allow people to cross-fertilize their thinking.

f. Have a laboratory, workshop, or "think tank" with necessary materials for tinkering, thinking, and planning.

g. Have performance reviews that support and encourage one's creative efforts, ideas, and actions.

h. Implement a policy that reduces fear of making a mistake if one tries something different.

i. Keep people openly informed about the problems in the organization that need solving.

j. Have a reward and recognition system for the creative person.

k. Have an outside person observe current organization functioning to assess creative output and suggest ways of improving innovation.

l. Have a team-development session with the special purpose of improving the creative atmosphere and output of the department or unit.

m. Rotate people into different positions or parts of the organization so there is a new mixture of people working on old problems.

n. Have a job enrichment session where people devise ways of enriching their own jobs.

3. *Implementing the plan.* After a plan of action has been developed it must be put into operation. If any of the above suggestions are combined into an action program, people must be willing to invest time and energy to try to ensure that new programs and actions have a fair chance to succeed.

4. *Assessing the plan.* After a new program has been functioning for a period of time, it is important to make an evaluation to see whether it is achieving the results desired. By such means as interviews, questionnaires, group discussions, and reaction panels, an assessment is made to see if the new actions have indeed resulted in a more creative organizational climate with an increase in the creative output of individuals and a more imaginative solution to problems.

References

Barron, Frank
  1969 *Creative Person and Creative Process.* New York: Holt, Rinehart and Winston, Inc.

122

Ghiselin, Brewster, ed.
  1952   *The Creative Process.* Berkeley: University of California Press.

Steiner, Gary
  1965   *The Creative Organization.* Chicago: University of Chicago Press.

OPEN-SYSTEM PLANNING

Most current research and theory about organizations is based on a closed-system model of the nature of the organization. For purposes of analysis, the organization is presumed to be contained within the confines of its physical operating structures. An automobile assembly plant, for example, is seen in the closed-system model as being a set of workers, in a particular location, producing cars. If something happens to reduce or restrict output, the diagnosis and change action generally take place within the confines of the plant where the workers are.

Almost all organization theorists, however, recognize that any organization is located in a wider environment and that it will be influenced considerably at times by conditions that occur outside its walls. The automobile plant will be affected by general economic conditions, government regulations on automotive safety and pollution-reducing equipment, demands of labor unions, availability and costs of raw materials, amount of the tax structure, price of the products of competitors, and on and on. In this sense the organization is an "open system." It is open to interaction with its wider environment and must plan its total effort to take into account the influences of external conditions. A more realistic way of thinking about an organization is illustrated in the diagram of the wider outside environment.

The outside environment supplies the inputs, which are processed or converted by the organization, via its throughput activities, into outputs, which go back into the environment and may subsequently alter or influence the new inputs, which again are funneled into the system. This is a continual, ongoing cycle for all organizations.

Wider Outside Environment

Organization			
Inputs → Throughputs → Outputs			
Wider Environment	**Inputs**	**Throughputs**	**Outputs**
1. Economic conditions 2. Competitors 3. Union demands 4. Tax structures 5. Government regulations 6. Consumer demands 7. Labor supply 8. Raw materials	1. Labor 2. Raw materials 3. Market information 4. Information about environment 5. Financial resources	1. Work flow 2. Administrative procedures and controls 3. Social system conditions 4. Management processes	1. Finished product 2. Terminated worker 3. Workers living in the community 4. Level of service 5. Company-community activities

The automobile plant must take in from the environment its supply of labor, raw materials, and equipment. In addition, if it is wise, it should seek out and take in all information possible about such external conditions as prices, markets, taxes, regulations, and the like, which must be considered in making all decisions — such as decisions about wages, cost of the product, kinds of dividends paid to investors, public relations activities, markets, and expansion or reduction possibilities. The internal or "closed" part of the organization then processes the inputs through its production setup — whether it be an assembly line, groups of craftsmen, or service departments — and transforms the inputs into some product or service that is returned again to the outside environment.

Every day sees a similar procedure: the workers come into the company from the outside environment and bring with them attitudes, reactions, feelings that may influence their work during the daily throughput activity. At the end of each day they go back into the community environment and discharge into it their feelings and reactions about the organization. If their feelings are positive, the community gets a constant supply of support for the notion that this is a good company. This in turn causes people to want to work for the company and use its products or services, and the resource loop is completed: what goes out eventually influences what comes in.

The Wider Environment inside an Organization

The above model looks at the whole organization as it is located in the total community or societal environment. In a similar sense, each department or subunit in a large organization could think of the total organization as its wider environment and could also begin to plan how to interact more effectively with the other parts of the total organization.

For example, a purchasing department has its larger environmental components within the company. It will be influenced by the policies, procedures, budgets, and constraints of other departments. Purchasing will take in as inputs requests for service from other departments, process those requests, and turn out as outputs a completed transaction of purchasing service. If the outputs are effective, the wider environment (other departments and management) will feel good and will continue to want to provide more inputs in the form of increased requests for more service. On the other hand, if the outputs are poor in quality, the inputs begin to decrease and the whole usefulness of the purchasing department is diminished.

Improving Effectiveness with the Outside Environment

Open-system planning is the term used to describe the process by which an organization or a subunit of an organization plans to improve its effectiveness in interaction with those parts of its wider environment essential for its continuous healthy functioning. Following are some of the important elements in effective open-system planning:

1. Identification and Specification of the "Core Mission"

Every organization (or unit) should have clearly defined for itself and its members what its basic goal, function, or "reason for being" is. It is difficult to know exactly how to relate to environmental demands unless the basic mission or purpose of the organization that needs to be protected and enhanced is clearly understood. Sometimes organizations spend too much time dealing with concerns not directly related to their core mission. For example, if a university defines its core mission as the training of undergraduates for effectively coping with modern society, university administrators may find, on closer examination, that they are spending too much time and effort in seeking and supporting research projects that have only a secondary influence on the core mission. Organizations need to put into priority listing expenditures of effort and resource in dealing with those parts of its environment that specifically affect their core mission. It is also possible that an organization has several parts to its core mission — some more important than others.

2. Identification of the Important Clients or Demand Systems

Having determined what the core mission is, those planning to deal with the outside environment need next to identify the individuals, groups, or organizations that represent important external clients (those using the products or services) and demand systems (those who have chosen to make demands of some kind on the organization).

The automobile plant may see as an important client all former buyers of their product and may see as a critical demand system the automobile workers' labor union. Both these parts of the wider environment need to be considered carefully as to the plans and programs used in trying to produce the best positive results. All clients and demand systems should be identified and then listed in order of importance as plans are made for further action.

3. "Is" and "Ought" Planning

Planners must first clearly describe "how it is" with each particular client and demand system. How are the relationships, the interactions, the amount of contact with that external unit? What about its responsiveness and reactions? The "is" of the current situation should be written down in detailed description. It may be important to gather current data from the client or demand systems so one can accurately understand how things really are.

After describing "how it is," the planner must then assess whether the current situation with that client or demand system is at the level the organization would prefer. If not, the planner must then clearly state how things "ought to be" if the relationship were at an optimum level.

4. Current Response to Clients and Demands

Having described how things are and how they ought to be, organization planners now describe in detail the current level of response to the client. Using accurate data as a base, they need to answer these questions: What does this client want from us? What are we currently doing to deal with him? Then follows the next question: Is our current response to the client or the demand moving us closer to where we would like to be?

5. Action Planning

Having determined how things ought to be and whether or not the current response is adequate, planners now decide what actions must be taken to achieve the desired state of affairs. The plan should include answers to these questions:
1. What actions must be taken to move in the desired direction?
2. Who should be taking this action?
3. What are the resource costs and allocations necessary?
4. What is the timetable for action? When should action start and finish?

5. How will we ensure follow-through? Who will need to report on progress? When will a progress report be due?

6. How will we evaluate or measure the action to be sure we are achieving our desired objectives?

Summary

Open-system planning is a method for consciously trying to change the responses and reactions of people or units outside the organization who are the users or influencers of the organization's outputs. Much current literature on management is centered in management of people and conditions *inside* the organization. Inside management will always be important, but any organization operates in some peril unless it has a conscious program for assessing its relationships with outside demands and spends time planning improvements in them.

References

Katz, Daniel, and Robert Kahn
  1966 *The Social Psychology of Organizations.* New York: John Wiley & Sons, Inc.

Letterer, Joseph
  1973 *The Analysis of Organizations.* New York: John Wiley & Sons, Inc.

MANIPULATIVE STRATEGIES*

In this age of enlightened management it may well be that the autocratic executive is beginning to experience an identity crisis following a training group experience, managerial training program, or the acquisition of an advanced degree in administration. Since the arrival of McGregor's *Human Side of Enterprise* (1960) more than a decade ago, few MBA graduates are not thoroughly knowledgeable about Theory-X and Theory-Y assumptions concerning human behavior in the industrial world. Having been exposed to modern theories of management, the autocratic administrator becomes well aware of the kind of executive he *should* be. This should-be image, however, may be incongruent with his want-to-be image as the man who runs a very tight, no-nonsense organization.

He is thus faced with a dilemma regarding the degree to which he should allow his subordinates to participate in managerial decisions. He is faced, on the one hand, with a desire to allow his underlings to become self-actualized in their respective organizational roles through exercising their own initiative and creative skills in making decisions and implementing them. On the other hand, he is confronted by the horrible thought that they might possibly make a wrong decision if left to their own devices.

Tannenbaum and Schmidt (1958:95–101) have proposed a useful model of participatory management which includes varying degrees of group involvement on a continuum ranging from very little to almost total group participation:

---

*With Spencer J. Condie.

1. Manager makes decision and announces it.
2. Manager "sells" decision.
3. Manager presents ideas and invites questions.
4. Manager presents tentative decision.
5. Manager presents problem, gets suggestions, makes decision.
6. Manager defines limits, asks group to make decision.
7. Manager permits subordinates to function within limits defined by superior.

For some leaders, managers, or executives, each of the above points on the continuum might represent alternative leadership *styles* or behavioral patterns congruent with their own personality and individual needs. For other individuals in superordinate positions, the continuum may represent alternative leadership *strategies*, or ways of getting people to do what you want them to do.

The Illusionary Democratic Leader

An all-too-frequent phenomenon is the leader who wishes to appear to have adopted a number 6 or 7 style in the Tannenbaum-Schmidt model but instead uses this style as a manipulative strategy. In reality he is operating at the number 1 level of decision-making participation. We shall refer to such a strategy as *illusionary democratic leadership*. In such a case the leader may present the parameters of a given problem and suggest some alternative solutions to the problem, the final solution of which is supposedly derived through group participation. However, in most cases the illusionary democratic leader will already have implemented the decision.

The Benevolent Autocrat

One of the earliest styles identified as a manipulative strategy is the *benevolent autocrat* (Bradford and Lippitt, 1945). This leader disguises his authoritarian bent in the form of the wise, kindly father who is only doing what he must do for "your good." Subordinates are thought of, and treated, as little children who are not yet mature enough to function independently and who therefore must be guided, directed, and protected from their own shortcomings.

The benevolent autocrat can be of two types: the autocratic leader who honestly believes that he is like a father to his subordinates and believes that his wisdom and experience entitle him to make decisions for others; or the person who adopts the paternalistic stance because it seems to put him out of reach of any adverse reaction. After all, who can attack daddy? This person assumes the kindly, benevolent pose but doesn't feel that way toward others. He finds it a more comfortable posture than taking the gloves off and demanding obedience and conformity.

The Pseudofamily

Gouldner (1950:644–59) has delineated a managerial strategy which centers around a series of actions taken on the part of the leader designed to create within the worker the feeling that he is part of a close-knit "family" unit and that the subordinate owes it to the unit to work hard in achieving organizational goals. He refers to this manipulative group cohesiveness as a "pseudo-*Gemeinschaft*" in that the leader is not genuinely concerned with building group integration but deliberately wants to create group identity so that he can use the group as a basis of influence and coercion.

In such a pseudo-*Gemeinschaft* the manager creates a false group feeling by (1) talking very personally to the workers in order to create the impression that they are all very close in their relationship; (2) engaging in personal favors which obligate his subordinates to do his bidding; (3) shifting members who resist his influence out of the group in a nonobvious way; (4) spending an inordinate amount of time being "around" people while subtly conveying his omnipresence; (5) instituting a system of reports under the guise of just wanting to know what is going on; and (6) keeping everyone busy even if the work isn't relevant or important.

The Leader with a Managerial Facade

A close relative to the above manager is the leader who adopts the Blake-Mouton *managerial facade* (1964:192–212). From a distrust of group decision-making ability the managerial facade strategist may "feel out positions and achieve commitment from those concerned, prior to assembling them." By composing a decision-making group exclusively of his allies, the manager is able to present the facade of allowing extensive participation and group involvement when, in fact, the outcome of such a group discussion was ensured prior to the group's inception.

The Phony Proposer

A variation on this same theme is the *phony proposer*, a person identified in research by Lawrence (1954). He is another under-the-skin autocrat who for some reason feels he must at least go through the motions of participatory management. His strategy is to present his own ideas to the group in the form of a proposal with a very obvious flaw in it. He supposes that as the group dutifully picks out the flaw and meticulously perfects the proposal they will achieve a sense of group fulfillment in achieving a decision together. Akin to this form of illusionary democracy is the person who offers two proposals, both of his own choosing, but asks the group to decide on

the final outcome. The catch is that one proposal is infinitely superior to the other, so that participation in the final decision can hardly be equated with involvement.

The Public Praiser

A style of manipulation that has been observed but not studied in depth is seen in the person who runs his operation his way by direct authority and control, but whenever he discusses his operation for public consumption via newspapers, radio, or television, he gives credit to "his wonderful team of cooperative assistants." As in all of the manipulative strategies, this form is designed to protect the autocrat from attack and criticism from others. If one has publicly declared that the results of the enterprise were from a team effort and credit and praise are given to others, what ungrateful person would then criticize the process? Reports from subordinates caught in situations with the public praiser indicate the ambivalence they feel toward him. They resent his autocratic methods but appreciate the public recognition. They also recognize that the public statements do not agree with the facts as they have experienced them, but since the publicity reflects favorably on them, it has some pleasing aspects.

The Impotent Committee

Another manipulative strategy is to create the impression that others are going to be involved in the planning or decision-making process by assigning work out to a committee. Some autocrats have all members of the organization on at least one committee, giving the false feeling that everyone will share in the developments of the organization. However, the leader so manipulates the use of the committee that the committee actions are never really implemented or have a chance to have impact.

There are a number of devices that can be used to make a committee impotent:

1. Committee reports must first be cleared through an "executive committee" which is controlled by the boss, and it is this executive group that has final authority.

2. The committee is asked to be a recommending body only, and then the votes are loaded to come out the way the leader wants.

3. Committees are not given adequate time to meet, resulting in inadequate work; so decisions must be made on a "crisis" basis with the excuse that "we just can't wait on the committee as much as we would like to."

4. Committee assignments are made so the critical areas are not turned over to a committee; the boss retains them himself and keeps committees involved in noncritical matters. It is also possible for the boss to place himself together with certain trusted lieutenants on the really critical committees so he can control the proposals that result.

Consequences of Manipulative Strategies

Observation and research have been done on the effects of manipulative strategies on peers and subordinates. More research is needed. However, it appears that one of the major consequences is the pushing of resistance to the manipulative leader down to a very covert, subtle level. Since there is the guise of participation and democracy, the person being manipulated feels guilty and off-balance if he confronts the leader. He knows that if he cites examples of manipulation the leader can cite examples of his apparent involvement of others. Thus the confrontation is "my opinion against yours," and the confronter fears that he will appear as a sorehead, an ingrate, or a power and status seeker. With resistance and negative reaction at an undercover level, it is difficult to deal with the negative effects of the leader. It often takes a skillful outsider to uncover the leadership style and its eroding effects.

In recent years considerable research has been directed toward that ancient breed of manipulators, the *Machiavellians* (Christie, 1970:82–86). As opposed to the autocratic leader who apparently has certain needs to dominate, the Machiavellian is an unabashed manipulator of superb expertise. The honest autocrat will read this paper and admit his propensities. He then may or may not alter his managerial style. The true Machiavellian, however, will read this article and chuckle to himself.

Conclusion

Regardless of one's personal needs or desires, if a leader cannot trust his subordinates with open participation in administrative decisions, he should at least spare them from the hypocrisy of illusionary democracy. Perhaps the autocratic executive must ease into a freer managerial style by allowing decisions of lesser import to be made by subordinates and then gradually delegating more and more authority to them. Upon evaluating the quality of their decisions, and after observing the valuable error-detection mechanism of group discussion, the executive may become aware of the tremendous potential creativity which he has unlocked in his underlings and himself as well.

References

Blake, Robert R., and Jane S. Mouton
   1964   *The Managerial Grid.* Houston: Gulf Publishing Company: 192–211.

Bradford, Leland P., and Ronald Lippitt
   1945   Building a democratic work group. *Personnel* 22(November): 143–44.

Christie, Richard
   1970   The Machiavellians among us. *Psychology Today* (November): 82–86.

Gouldner, Alvin W. (ed.)
   1950   *Studies in Leadership: Leadership and Democratic Action.* New York: Harper & Row Publishers: 644–59.

Lawrence, Paul
   1954   How to deal with resistance to change. *Harvard Business Review* (May-June): 56.

McGregor, Douglas
   1960   *The Human Side of Enterprise.* New York: McGraw-Hill.

Tannenbaum, Robert T., and Warren H. Schmidt
   1958   How to choose a leadership pattern. *Harvard Business Review* (March-April): 95–101.

CONFLICT*

One of the common clichés of our time is that "we live in a complex society." This statement is used in a variety of contexts, but it often is used philosophically to explain conditions that are bewildering and confusing. Others nod wisely and sympathetically in agreement. Like many clichés, the statement is essentially correct, but it offers no real insight. Recent explorations in theory and research in the behavioral sciences, especially role theory, offer some real insights into conditions that produce the almost helpless explanation: "We live in a complex society."

Nearly all persons observe that, as they move from one situation or set of relationships to another, their behavior changes. One does not behave the same way in church as he does at work, at home, at a party, or at a lodge meeting. Each situation makes specific demands to which most people readily respond. In social science parlance each different set of responses is a *role* — that behavior which is expected in a given situation. Complexity and confusion come as people multiply the number of roles they must assume without recognizing the forces at work.

First, it is important to note that in each situation where one assumes a role, others involved in the situation have at their disposal the power to reward or punish him to the degree he fulfills or fails to fulfill his role obligations. If a subordinate does not fulfill his work role properly (carrying out assignments, getting work done on time),

---

*Revised. Reprinted by special permission from *Adult Leadership*. William G. Dyer, "Looking at Conflict," (September 1960).

135

his boss may apply certain punishments by a reprimand or denying certain benefits or rewards.

Second, it should be recognized that most people internalize the demands of the role; that is, the expected role behavior becomes a part of the need system of the individual. In order to maintain his self-respect, his respect from others, his feelings of adequacy and self-worth, he needs to perform the roles he has accepted. If a person who has internalized a role does not conform to the demands of the role, he is afflicted with self-punishment — feelings of guilt or self-effacement — even though there is no other person present to apply an external punishment. Thus a boy who drinks with the gang and wins their approval will suffer pangs of guilt from knowing he has violated the demands of his role as a church member. A salesman who pads his expense account because others do it feels a loss of self-respect because his action is a violation of what he feels a truly honest person would do.

Punishment or reward, then, may stem from other persons or from within oneself. People are generally very sensitive to their own reactions and try consciously or unconsciously to maintain themselves in an overall condition where there is a maximum of reward and a minimum of punishment. One must recognize, of course, that individuals differ in their definitions of reward and punishment.

Problems and conflict arise when a person is caught in a situation where, by performing a role, he brings upon himself *both* reward and punishment. This is the basis of role conflict. Role conflict can be divided into two general classes: conflict of multiple roles and conflict internal to one role. These can, in turn, be subdivided. Conflicts between roles can be a conflict of norms or a conflict of time. Conflict within a role can be conflict of time, of needed ability, or of expectations.

Multiple-role Conflict

Disparity between Group Norms

A common source of serious conflict lies in the disparity between the demands of two roles one person is expected to take. A teenager often finds that his role in his peer group demands different behavior from that demanded by his role at home or as a church member. To steal hubcaps may elicit the approval of the gang, but it brings swift disapproval from the parent or the minister. Research evidence has documented the dilemmas of the foreman who finds himself caught between the demands of his old group of worker friends and his new role as a representative of management.

Essentially the conflict arises because of group norms, from which the roles are derived. The norms of group A may demand certain actions, and the norms of group B may pressure for behavior

diametrically opposed. This involves not only conflicting pressures from others, but also personal conflict in the individual who may be personally oriented to both sets of norms. Thus, he has guilt feelings when he behaves one way even if persons in the other group do not know of his "deviant" behavior.

This type of conflict is found among many people: a business-man caught between accepted cutthroat business practices and Christian ethics insisting that he love his neighbor as himself; a student pressured by classmates to cheat — in conflict with home and church norms; or a member of a Republican family who belongs to a Democratic social group.

How do people handle this type of role conflict? Obviously not everyone in this conflict of multiple roles cracks up under the strain. A number of psychologically protective devices are used. Some use various defense mechanisms, such as rationalization or repression. Others compartmentalize; that is, they put each role in a separate mental compartment and refuse to see any conflict. A fortunate few are able to make a decision to withdraw from one of the conflict groups in light of some priority of values. Many continue to operate within a system of stress, anxiety, pressure, and guilt feelings, being unable to eliminate either of the conflicting roles.

"Time Crunch"

Time conflict is another type of multiple-role conflict. This conflict is the common phenomenon in which a person assumes so many roles in so many groups that he cannot possibly fulfill all the obligations involved. As a result each group is applying pressures to get the person to involve himself in its activity. A person in this situation may receive rewards from one group for spending his time with their program while he receives negative pressures from another group for not having spent time with them. The classic example is the man who moves ahead professionally but receives negative reactions from his family for being gone so much.

In this type of conflict a person is under constant pressure to perform each of the many roles demanding attention. Knowing this, each group tries to apply the most pressure, vying for the participation of the overloaded person. Fortunate is he who can evaluate his many roles and eliminate or redefine some of them to reduce the conflict and tension level.

Internal Role Conflict

Time

Conflict also occurs within a single role, and the time factor again is involved. It is closely tied with the matter of multiple group membership, for a person may accept a role only to find that he really does not have time to meet its demands and does not know how to get out of it.

Lack of Needed Ability

Internal role conflict may also be caused by a lack of necessary ability. In this case a person accepts a role for which he has time and for which there is no conflict with any other role and then discovers that it demands actions which he feels he does not have the ability to fulfill. A person too shy and retiring to refuse a role as fund-raiser in an organization may be terrified at the prospect of visiting people to ask them for money. The role hangs over his head like an awesome burden, and he may think of all kinds of reasons why he doesn't have time to carry out the assignment, or he may complete the task, detesting it all the time and refusing to do anything in the organization again.

From this analysis one would naturally assume that the wisest course would be to match role demands with skills and ability. This is easier said than done. On the one hand, it is possible that a person may have the latent ability and could grow with the job even though he feels inadequate. On the other hand, a person may be over-confident and willing to accept but not be competent in actual performance.

The acceptance of a role for which a person feels he does not have the necessary ability may result in his receiving certain rewards from the group, but accompanying it are feelings of self-torture and pressures which are very real and very painful.

Failure to Fulfill Others' Expectations

Finally, there is the situation where a person finds himself in conflict because of different people's having differing expectations as to how his role should be carried out. A teacher may find that some parents expect her to be a strict disciplinarian, and others feel she should be very permissive and accepting. By performing her role one way she receives the approval of one set of parents but the angry reactions of the other. A reversal of behavior does not remove her from the conflict. This type of conflict is even more frustrating when people do not define their expectations of the role, so that the person is the recipient of negative reactions without knowing what he has done to elicit them. A person new to the management position often experiences this kind of conflict. His boss may expect one type of performance as his peer group puts on subtle pressure for contrary actions. His wife may have a widely differing conception of his manager's role, and his former teachers may have taught him yet another view. Finally, those who are his subordinates have their views as to how he should function.

It is obviously impossible to meet everyone's expectations when they are all different. The old tale of the couple and the donkey illustrates the point graphically. In trying to meet everyone's expectations, the couple wound up carrying the donkey — a ridiculous adjustment to the situation. It is also apparent that this type of conflict is difficult to resolve, especially when each faction feels its expectations are legitimate. Sometimes it is possible to change people's expectations. Sometimes one needs to perform the role as he thinks it should be done despite the demands of others. This latter action lessens one's inner conflicts but does not eliminate the external pressures.

If we put together all the possible types of role-conflict situations mentioned above, it becomes apparent that this is indeed a "very complex society." Imagine a person who has too many roles, some of which represent opposing group norms, some of which demand actions for which he has inadequate skills, and some of which represent responses to conflicting expectations. In each case others are applying constant pressures, trying to get him to fulfill the role as the organization defines it, and at the same time the person himself is suffering from feelings of inadequacy and guilt. With this insight the cliché is no longer an insipid comment, but a serious reflection of today's reality.

How to Minimize Role Conflict

A person who experiences role conflict in any of its forms may need assistance in sorting out his roles and making decisions as to priorities and actions. It is impossible to work out conflicts until one has clearly described what his goals are. Goal setting is the first step. Following that it is possible to establish priorities which will help in reducing time conflicts. If one also establishes a list of groups or systems according to priority, problems of expectations may get sorted out.

Values are also important. Role conflicts will continue until one has clearly determined what his values are — what is valuable and what is not. Conflict resolution goes deep, for a person must wrestle with such fundamental issues as: What are my goals? What are my values? What are my priorities? Following this he may deal with matters of taking risks, saying no, and taking positive action to bring order out of a world of conflict.

References

Kahn, Robert, et al.
   1964   *Organizational Stress: Studies in Role Conflict and Ambiguity.* New York: John Wiley and Son.

Wolfe, Donald, and J. Diedrick Snork
   1962   A study of tensions and adjustment under role conflict. *Journal of Social Issues* 18, no. 3: 102–21.

CULTURAL BARRIERS*

The movement emphasizing group-centered leadership is finding popular acceptance in educational, industrial, and religious circles. The trend still meets resistance from some persons or groups whose orientation to certain other cultural trends causes them to view with hostility and suspicion this move toward participative action.

Basic to the participative group approach to leadership is the idea that all group members should work together on the problem at hand and have a share in the decision-making process. Shared action requires that each member of the group be considered as individually important. His ideas and contributions must be seen as important to the overall functioning of the group. It is apparent that this process increases the democratic nature of group action, for in a democracy each person is considered equal and each person's ideas are equated with everyone else's.

This idea of democratic procedure has long and deep roots in American culture. Americans are fond of quoting from the Declaration of Independence that "all men are created equal." There are, however, other cultural roots, just as deep and strong, that create barriers to participative action.

This discussion points out some of these resistant factors so that they may more intelligently be understood and handled. It should be noted that different groups, sections of the country, and social strata exhibit these characteristics in differing degrees. Thus the

---

*Revised. Reprinted by special permission from *Adult Leadership*. William G. Dyer, "Cultural barriers to leadership," (January 1959).

141

barriers to participative action and the method of handling the barriers will change as one shifts from place to place.

Barrier One: Sex Roles

Although the status of women has been raised considerably in the United States in the past forty years, there is still a strong patriarchal tradition existing in many parts of the country. This tradition emphasizes the "natural" superiority of the male with his right to ultimate powers in decision making. Women as well as men operate in this tradition. Many women in mixed groups feel it is the natural prerogative of the men to assume authority and make final decisions. In many groups this leads to a domination of the group by men. There are often feelings of resentment on the part of some men, and women too, when some women voice their ideas with vigor and expect equal opportunities in group activities.

Accompanying this idea of traditional male authority is the feeling held by many that there are certain areas that are in the domain of the male (this may also operate in reverse fashion). Some men will operate in democratic fashion with women in some areas, but when it comes to other subjects — often politics, sports, sex, money matters — these are considered "man's talk." A woman, no matter how competent, has difficulty making a contribution. The current movement for equality between the sexes has improved some situations but created "backlash" conditions in others.

Barrier Two: Prestige

It appears to be a rather natural thing to accord more prestige, deference, and authority to those persons who have acquired more of certain items that are held in esteem in our culture. We tend to look up to those persons who have greater experience, age, education, money, and/or social position. Not only do many people who are lacking in these areas feel inadequate to talk on an equal basis with the more favorably endowed, but they also feel that these people have a natural right to occupy positions of dominance. They may feel it presumptuous of themselves to question, criticize, or comment. Then, too, many higher-status people agree that they should be accorded more prestige and authority.

Some people will be able to make a superior contribution in certain areas because of a higher degree of competence. However, one person is seldom, if ever, superior in all areas, and there is no reason why he should be constantly accorded or should assume positions of authority. We often find people who make a claim to positions of dominance because of greater age, and our cultural patterns support

this idea of respect and deference both to parents and to other older people.

When people have wealth or social position, they are often accorded higher status than is warranted by their objectively considered competency, knowledge, or skills. These feelings of superiority or inferiority are real blocks to effective participation.

Barrier Three: Formal Status

Closely allied to barrier two is the matter of a formal status hierarchy found in many organizations. Many of them have a division of labor and authority ranked very precisely in terms of offices ranging from president on down to supervisors, foremen, and finally to workers or lay members. Such an organization is found in most businesses, schools, churches, and government agencies.

When people of varying ranks get together, those in the lower positions often feel a great reluctance to participate as equals. A second lieutenant does not easily offer criticism of the policies of the base commander, nor does a file clerk or bank teller feel free to discuss openly and equally his views of the company with the president. The feeling that one's job may be in jeopardy if he violates the rules or expectations of the higher-status person reduces many people to the role of "yes-men." The reverse also occurs — a higher-status person may resent the equal participation of a lower-ranking person. He might perceive this participation as a threat to his own position or feel that those in authority over him disapprove of such action.

Barrier Four: Formal Leadership

A most common barrier to equality of group action is the persistent cultural norm concerning the necessity and desirability of every group's having a formal leader. Even in groups where the first three barriers may not be present — a group of the same sex, equal prestige, and organizational status — a common procedure is to elect one person the formal leader and consciously or unconsciously endow him with greater powers than the rest.

This should not be confused with the desirability of having a formal leader who performs certain useful functions for the group, such as calling the meeting to order, setting the agenda, and operating as a mediator for discussion. What is meant here is the too often accepted assumption by both the group members and the formally appointed leader that once a person has been appointed a formal leader he has greater insights, abilities, powers of discernment and analysis, and wisdom than the other members.

In such cases the formal leader tends to dominate the meeting, initiate more action, and is looked upon as being the final authority. In reality the group as a whole probably possesses all these qualities to a greater degree than does the one leader.

Barrier Five: Prejudice

One of the most prevalent of the forces resistant to democratic action is prejudice. Our culture helps maintain and perpetuate prejudice through the establishing of certain discriminatory practices handed down from parent to child as part of his cultural inheritance.

Prejudice is a strong, persistent emotional attitude toward any object. We think most often in terms of racial or religious prejudice, but one may have feelings of prejudice against other persons because of such factors as politics, occupation, family background, or place of origin. These feelings of prejudice constantly interfere with productive, effective group action. Good communication is interrupted in the group as persons listen and respond through their screen of prejudice. Often people fail to listen to or immediately reject the ideas of a person because of *who* the person is rather than *what* he says.

Prejudice may result in discrimination in the group as persons are left off committees, assigned to routine or drudgery tasks, not allowed to assume positions of responsibility, or even completely ignored. Thus they are unable to enrich the group with their personal resources.

Through the years it has become culturally acceptable to react in prejudiced ways toward certain kinds of people, particularly those in minority groups. As a result, persons who interrupt the group with acts of prejudice may find the weight of cultural practice in their favor. Those who may object to their behavior often allow it to persist because "everyone does it" or "that's the way lots of people feel." Thereby they contribute to the continuation of prejudice and discrimination.

How to Overcome the Barriers

One might well ask here, "What can be done to eliminate or diminish these barriers in our group?" The solutions are more easily listed than accomplished. It should be remembered that people hold the above attitudes as a result of early and persistent cultural conditioning. And, while one group may wish to change attitudes, there are other groups to which these people belong that foster and encourage barrier attitudes. One should not expect to effect immediate change, for attitudes change slowly at best. However, we might well remember the following suggestions:

1. Examine Our Own Behavior

Do we create barriers to democratic action in our group because we persist in some of the practices listed above? The two areas of change are change in oneself and change in others. Awareness that one holds certain attitudes is the first step in changing them.

2. Discuss These Barriers Openly and Frankly in the Group

This, of course, assumes that the emotional climate of the group is such that these matters may be freely and openly discussed without creating more problems than are solved. If, however, the group as a whole recognizes the problem, each person may help the others in the group.

3. Give Warm Acceptance to the Person Who Holds Barrier Attitudes

Attitude change is most effectively produced by one's friends in warm, primary-type relationships. Rejection of the prejudiced person is not the answer. Rejection not only prohibits the rejected one from making a contribution to the group but often reinforces the very attitudes we wish to change.

4. Adopt the Idea of Trying Out New Things

It is easier to change if we have had a good experience in the new procedure or behavior pattern we are considering adopting. If any of the above barriers exist in your group, consciously try out the reverse procedure; for example, let the women present the program on politics; assign an important task to the lowest-status person; put a subordinate at the head of a committee composed of his superiors; try operating without a formal leader. These new experiences carried out in an atmosphere of friendliness and acceptance can help us get new perspectives.

5. Have Periodic Sessions of Evaluation and Analysis of the Group

We need to assess constantly in order to be sure that new barriers are not being introduced into our group.

References

Diedrich, Richard, and Allan Dye
  1972 *Group Procedures.* Boston: Houghton Mifflin Co.

Kemp, Gratton
  1964 *Perspectives on the Group Process.* Boston: Houghton Mifflin Co.

DECISION
TO FAIL*

If someone were asked if he wanted to make sure he would fail in any given venture, his response would be an indignant *no*. He would insist all his efforts were directed toward succeeding. The fact remains that many people cause their own defeat as surely as if they had made a conscious decision to fail. For whatever reason, they give up their right to success as though failure were their goal.

The Trip to Abilene: A Modern Parable

A young man and his bride are visiting her folks in the town of Coleman, Texas. Coleman is in the middle of the plains, and the wind blows, and it gets hot. It is the middle of the summer, and there is not much to do in Coleman, a town of about five thousand people. The young man, his wife, and the parents-in-law are sitting around on a Sunday afternoon, drinking lemonade and playing dominoes. From all appearances, the family is having a good time, when suddenly and surprisingly the father-in-law says, "Why don't we all get dressed and drive to Abilene, and have dinner in the cafeteria?" The young man thinks to himself, "Good night! There is nothing I would like to do less than to drive to Abilene." Abilene is fifty-three miles from Coleman, over a winding road. He knows that the automobile does not have air conditioning, and in order to keep the wind from blowing the dust into the automobile, they will have to drive with the windows up. He also knows that the only place to eat that is open in Abilene on a Sunday afternoon is the Good Luck Cafeteria. The food at the Good Luck Cafeteria leaves much to be desired, but he thinks, "If my father-in-law wants to go to Abilene, I guess it's all right."

---

*With Jerry B. Harvey.

So he says, "That sounds fine to me. I mean if Beth (his wife) wants to go."

And she says, "Well, yes, if everyone wants to go to Abilene, that's fine — if Mother really wants to go."

Mother replies, "Oh, yes, if you all want to go, well, that's where I want to go."

They all put on their Sunday clothes, climb into the old Buick, and take a long, hot, dusty trip to Abilene. When they arrive there, sure enough, the only place open is the Good Luck Cafeteria. They have a greasy meal, crowd into the automobile, and drive fifty-three miles home.

Finally, worn out, hot, tired, dusty, irritable, they struggle back into the house, find another glass of lemonade, and the father-in-law says, "Boy, am I glad that's over! If there's anything I didn't want to do, it was to go to Abilene. I sure wouldn't have gone, if you three hadn't pressured me into it!"

The son-in-law says, "What do you mean, you didn't want to go to Abilene? And what do you mean, we pressured you into it? I only went because the rest of you wanted to go. I didn't pressure anybody."

His wife speaks up, "What do you mean? I didn't want to go to Abilene. The only reason I went was because you, Mama, and Daddy wanted to go."

Mother chimes in, "I didn't want to go to Abilene. That's the last place in the world I wanted to go. I only went because Father and the two of you said you wanted to go."

Father expands on his previous statement, "As I said before, I didn't want to go to Abilene. I just suggested going because I was afraid everybody was really bored sitting around playing dominoes, and I thought you might prefer to do something else. I was just sort of making conversation, hoping you'd suggest something better, but I really didn't expect you to take me up on my idea."

And so we have an interesting paradox: four reasonably intelligent people all combining to do something that none of them wanted to do in the first place. In fact, as a paradox within a paradox, you might say that this inability to cope with agreement (that is, the hidden agreement that they didn't want to go to Abilene) was the basic cause of their dilemma.

This is the parable. As with any parable there may be many interpretations and many lessons to be learned. You might see something about a problem in communication. You might detect an element of fear. You might even see some concern about love. It is also possible to draw some conclusions about integrity. Of central concern is an action in which each of us individually and collectively may engage from time to time — that is, taking an unwanted trip to Abilene. In fact, one of the primary functions of effective management of families, churches, businesses, and governments is to keep people from taking a dusty trip to Abilene and eating a greasy meal at the Good Luck Cafeteria. Stated differently, there are many different kinds of trips to Abilene, and following are just a few that might be possible at the personal, interpersonal, and organizational levels.

Personal Decisions to Fail

Some decisions to fail occur as people make critical life choices — for example, as they choose a life's companion. Consider a young man and a young woman who have been going together for some time and are planning to be married. If you were to interview each one of them separately and privately and ask, "How do you feel about this person you have selected?" they might answer something like this: "Honestly, now that you have asked, I really feel deep down that he (she) isn't the right person. There are a lot of things we don't share or do or understand or like about each other." Unfortunately, like many couples wanting to bolster a sagging relationship, they sometimes move to more and more demands for personal intimacy. Expectations are built up among themselves, their family, and their friends until it becomes difficult — at least in their minds — to terminate the relationship. Both have made the declaration to marry, although neither really wants to or feels it is the "right" thing to do. The girl thinks, "He is expecting to go through with this." The boy says to himself, "I am sure she is planning the wedding." If you ask them, "What are you going to do about this situation?" they will probably say, "We are going to announce our wedding date next week." This young couple would be in danger of taking a tragic trip to Abilene by doing something that neither wants to do and by engaging in an activity and making a crucial decision that neither feels is appropriate. One might say they are making a decision to fail.

Another kind of trip to Abilene might involve the choosing of an occupation or a life-style. Such a choice may be yet another way of taking a trip to Abilene. For example, you might talk to a recent college graduate and ask, "What do you want to do, now that you have your degree?"

If he searched deep within, he might say, "You know, what I would really like to do is to go buy a farm, raise some cattle, teach high school, and work in the boy scouts."

"What are you going to do?"

"Well, next week I am going to Los Angeles to accept a job in the aerospace industry."

If he carries through with such a decision, he will for all intents and purposes consign himself to an endless series of meals at the Good Luck Cafeteria.

Not all students make such a poor choice. Recently, for instance, a student who had received an MBA degree wrote a letter to his professor. He described finishing his degree, and he said, "I was at this time contemplating traveling to any number of metropolitan areas to find work since my search at school left me jobless. Instead I took a construction job in Grand Teton National Park with hopes in mind

149

of being able to latch onto something in that area. At the summer's end I received an offer and took a job in park management, still in Grand Teton. I have had a chance to think throughout the quiet winter evenings, and I realize that I am much happier than I would have been surrounded by the noise and bustle of city life. I have also come to realize that I just was not cut out for the keen competitive life of high finance and am thoroughly enjoying the more leisurely approach to life that is offered in the National Park Service. Being located in an area that is only five miles from work and less than fifty yards from the woods makes up whatever else might be lacking in the way of culture and erstwhile eases of life that are found in the larger areas." Here is at least one young man who avoided a dusty trip to Abilene.

Not everyone need live on the farm or in the woods to avoid that miserable trip. There are some who, if they were to search the deeper recesses of their own thoughts and aspirations, would say, "I really want to be a writer," or "I have the capability of being a top-flight scientist. I really should get a Ph.D." But their trip to Abilene is taking the nearest, most available job at the best salary. They are in danger of arriving at Abilene, a place where they don't want to be, joining the fellow in the aerospace industry for a greasy meal at the Good Luck Cafeteria.

Interpersonal Decisions to Fail

Married couples may find themselves on the road to Abilene as they begin to move in directions that neither really wants. If you were to talk to each of them privately, the interviews would go something like this:

To the young wife, "How do you feel about your relationship?"

"I'm not satisfied or happy."

"What's the matter?"

"We don't do a lot of things together. We are drifting away from our basic values. We tend to bicker and quarrel and fight with each other more than we should."

"You're not satisfied with that?"

"No, I don't like it at all."

Likewise, if you talk with the young husband, you would probably hear the same thing: "I don't like it. I'm not satisfied with what we are doing. I don't really like the direction we are taking. It isn't what I want."

"What are you going to do about it?"

"Well, we'll probably sit in the front room and quarrel and fight, and go to bed and sulk."

Such a young couple is indeed taking a trip to Abilene when Salt Lake City or San Bernardino is where they would rather be.

In a striking piece of research in the field of social psychology, a professor at Yale, Stanley Milgram, represents what can be a dangerous kind of trip to Abilene for anyone. He decided to investigate the possibility that people give up their responsibility for decisions to others in positions of authority. To test his basic hypothesis, he invited college students into a laboratory. As each one arrived, he would see a man seated in what appeared to be an electric chair with electrodes attached to his body. (What the students didn't know was that the chair was a fake; no electricity actually came in.) The experimenter would announce, "We want to see how much electric shock this person can take. Would you sit down at the control board and manipulate a central knob which will shock the person with increasing amounts of electricity."

The student would sit down, and the experimenter would say, "Turn the switch." The student would turn the switch. A light would go on in front of the person in the electric chair, and he would begin to scream and writhe in pretended pain. The student could see and hear him. He would look up, and the experimenter would say, "That's all right, he can take more. Give him some more." The student would turn the knob more, and the person in the chair would yell and scream harder and louder. Again the student would look up, and the experimenter would say, "That's all right. He can take more. Give it to him." A large percentage of students would continue to turn the knob more and more, even though they could see and hear the apparent evidence of their own actions.

When the experiment was over, the interviewers talked to them and asked, "Why did you do it? Didn't you see the person was in pain?"

"Yes, I saw that," was the common answer.

"Why did you continue?"

The reply was simple: "It wasn't my experiment. After all, it was the psychologist who was in charge. I figured he knew that he was doing, so I just followed what he said."

Any time any person violates his own conscience, his own values, and begins to engage in behavior that he personally does not feel is right or conscionable or appropriate, he is in danger of taking a terrible trip to Abilene.

Organizational Decisions to Fail

Trips to Abilene occur at the organization level, too. For example, a consultant to a large eastern corporation found that the company had committed several million dollars to the development of a new product. In interviewing almost all the people in top positions in the corporation, he found that everyone was worried about the research program. The multimillion dollar investment represented an important corporate outlay. From the top to the bottom he found each person saying the same thing, "I think the research program is a fiasco, an unwise investment of money. It isn't going to produce what we think it is."

"What are you going to do about it?"

"We just had a meeting, and we are going to commit another million and a half to the research program." Each person sat in his corporate office, afraid of what might happen if he spoke up and expressed his objections. Each thought that everybody else was for the project. There was a great deal of collective ignorance, and nobody was willing to stand forth and express clearly and soundly what he honestly felt. As a result, the corporation nearly took a trip to corporate bankruptcy in Abilene.

Fear of Admitting the Truth

We find trips to Abilene at the corporate level, the family, and the individual level. Why do they occur? What is it that causes people to marry people they don't love, take jobs they don't like, and support projects doomed to failure? Stated differently, why do they make decisions to fail? Underlying all such decisions are fear and fantasy — the fear of what might happen if one speaks up and voices the truth as he sees it. What will people say if we break our engagement? What will my wife say if I admit that I haven't been planning the kind of family life I think she wants? What will everyone say if I don't go ahead and take the job in Chicago? What will happen to me if I stand up and declare that the last decision we made in our organization was dangerously speculative? What will happen to me if I go against a prevailing political opinion? The fear of what might happen, the fantasy of what might come tumbling down around us if we don't keep our mouths closed, can put us in danger of climbing into a car and taking a long dusty trip to Abilene when we would much prefer to be in New Orleans.

How to Avoid Trips to Abilene

Since a major problem in making decisions to fail is that each of us is unaware of the real feelings of others, it is important that someone take enough risk to voice his concerns and put them out in the open before others.

Regardless of whether the person is in a business organization, a family, or a church, he must accept the consequences of his risk. Others, hearing his declaration of what he honestly feels, may too be encouraged to overcome their fears and fantasies. As a result of the new, honest information, all may find they are on a road none wants to travel, and they may therefore have the opportunity to reverse their course in a direction they really want to take.

It is also possible the person raising the issue for open consideration may find that there is real disagreement with his concern, and in that case he may set his fears at rest. There is also the possibility that the others are so afraid to reverse their previous decisions that they will react negatively to the person who has raised their secret fears to the level of discussion and examination. He may be penalized in some way, or even rejected. But at the same time he will be forced to move in directions that express his honest commitments.

The consultant or change agent or manager who discovers the dynamics of hidden agreement inherent to the Abilene paradox will serve his client best by bringing all parties together and identifying for everyone the major agreements he has heard. He may even describe the Abilene parable and ask those present if the data he has gathered represent such a possibility for them. Having surfaced the basic agreements, the change agent tries to help the client to reduce anxiety stemming from phantom fear and fantasies which block problem solving, to come to grips with making decisions and taking the actions that such honest agreement requires. In summary, by focusing on hidden agreements, the consultant helps his client reach conclusions that succeed rather than decisions that fail.

Reference

Harvey, Jerry B.
  1974   The Abilene paradox. *Organization Dynamics* (Summer): 63–80.

TRAINING

Training programs are an important set of activities in many organizations. Through these programs the effectiveness of people at all levels is hopefully increased. Training directors and specialists are professionals whose job it is to plan and carry out training programs that will make a difference. Since a training program can be time-consuming and expensive and still not produce results, the nature of effective training needs to be examined.

Training, as presently used, refers to any type of education program that leads to an improvement of performance by a person or persons engaged in an ongoing activity. Underlying the idea of training is the assumption that people can change behavior and that for various reasons (to be discussed) people should engage in activities that will lead to an improvement of performance.

Improvement is generally seen as behavior or performance that is more efficient — gets more output with less expenditure of resources — or more effective — achieves goals with "better" (qualitatively) results. In the case of managers, training in the first sense might make the manager more efficient; that is, he might be taught to organize his time in such a way that he accomplishes the same amount of work in less time. Or he might become more effective; that is, he might be taught to handle counseling problems in such a way that people feel better about being helped after seeing him.

When to Train People

The question of when to begin training should be thought about seriously. We have a general cultural value which says that everyone

155

can improve himself, that no one is perfect. Implicit in this idea is the notion that everyone could, with benefit, go through some training concerning every facet of his life. This orientation, taken to its absurd limits, would finally result in everyone's spending all his time in some type of "training." These are the important questions: Is there some level of performance (either a minimum level or an optimum level) that people should achieve? If they have not reached this level, should some type of training be instigated?

Usually organizations have not thought through what levels or limits should be reached through training. But since we believe in improvement, all kinds of training programs are constantly being initiated with the hope that they will do some good. This also suggests that most training programs have little or no evaluation attached to them to determine if the training has accomplished its proposed goals.

1. If realistic performance levels have been established, however, and if people have not achieved these levels, some type of training would seem to be appropriate.

2. Training is also seen as necessary as a means of improving performance when a person is inexperienced in the role or job demands. Thus a person new to a position often goes through a training program as the educative means of preparing him to perform his job at the required level.

When Not to Train People

Despite the cultural value that anyone can improve, there are probably times when training should not be utilized:

1. The time taken for the training program would not be worth the benefits that would accrue.

2. The beneficial results of the training program are questionable.

3. The training program would result in behavior change that really is not functional.

4. More effective results can be achieved by simpler methods (less time-consuming, less costly).

In a managers' program, we might try to train all managers in the art of counseling when it would actually be simpler to redefine the manager's job as that of referring people with counseling problems to a trained professional. Of course, there would have to be provision made for trained counselors on an organizational basis.

Types of Training Programs

In attempts to bring about an improvement of performance, a great many actions are taken. Some common actions and their limitations are the following:

Structured Learning Programs

Trainers hope that people reading or listening to descriptions of new ways of behaving will understand them well enough and be sufficiently motivated that they will begin to try out the new behaviors on their own. The problems here are those of communication, understanding, and motivation. It is hard to determine whether people reading or hearing material really understand it the way the author intended. It is even more difficult to know whether they are capable of putting into action the kind of performance the author intended.

Inherently weak by itself, this kind of program needs support to help people understand what is presented and begin to put it into action.

Training Meetings, Programs, Conferences

There is a wide variety of training programs. The poorest merely bring people together and in a variety of ways (lectures, films, tapes, handout materials) tell them what they ought to be doing. Trainers then hope they will do what they have been told.

The best programs do the following:

1. Allow people to talk about and explore the reasons for their current performance.

2. Allow them to set their own goals for improved performance.

3. Allow them to try out and practice new ways of behaving to gain some experience with new behaviors.

4. Provide feedback on the effectiveness of new behaviors.

All programs, both good and bad, have the problem of learning transfer. Whenever we take people off the job and try to train them for that job in a program setting, we face the problem that they may behave very well in the safe program, but when they return to the real situation, the press of many forces causes them to revert back to old ways of behaving. A good deal of research has indicated that people need to have some support and encouragement in the ongoing situation in order to be successful in trying out and continuing new behaviors. Training seems best done in the actual work setting so that transfer problems are essentially eliminated.

Coaching

Coaching is an old principle of training and derives from the notion of the athletic coach who practices his players during the week, watches the performance during the game, takes people out of the game, gives them instructions, and then puts them back into the game. Following the game, they have a critique of performance, more practice, and another game.

This is an old principle, but it is losing ground. In many situations it is not easy to have a coach present watching the performance and giving new instructions. Even so, many organizations are trying

types of coaching; some are assigning new men to experienced older men who act as coaches for a period of training. A major activity of an effective manager is to coach his subordinates.

Consultants

A type of coach is the consultant who comes from outside the organization; watches the ongoing performance; and then gives instruction, guidance, directions, and practice sessions in an attempt to help improve the performance level.

Job Rotation

Somewhat akin to coaching is job rotation, where a person who must supervise a wide variety of people and positions spends some time in each job, so that he has some specific firsthand experience, hopefully under the coaching of a qualified person.

Qualities of a Good Training Program

Having examined a number of aspects of training and training programs, we need to spell out what constitutes a good training program.

Examination of Performance

A good training program will include an opportunity for the trainee to examine his current performance level in such a way that he clearly sees what he is doing that is effective and what needs improving. An important aspect of this process is feedback — the receiving of data from others as to how he is doing in his job. In order to examine his performance, he needs a process of data collection; feedback is one aspect of this process. One weakness of many training programs is that trainees often are not really sure what they need to improve; there has been little or no collection of data or feedback about their performance.

Establishment of Change Goals

If a person is to improve his performance, he needs to know what he is currently doing, and he needs to decide himself what his goals for improvement are. To make such a decision, he must know his own potentials and limitations so that he can set realistic goals for himself. To be truly motivated, a person must supply his own motivation out of his own set of commitments. Motivation and commitment are less if someone else establishes the change goals and tries to get a person to change when he has no real involvement in the change process.

New Information, Ideas, Principles, Directions

Once a person sees what he has been doing that needs improving and has set some goals for his own improvement, he can use new ideas, new directions, and new principles. Until the first two conditions have been met, it is hard for him to know whether he really needs new information or how to use it after he gets it. Too many programs consist of funneling new information to people before they have any real feel for how they can use it effectively in their programs.

Experimentation and Practice

People do not change easily or all at once. Most of us need to have a chance to try out new ways, to become familiar with new procedures, to go through them several times to feel comfortable with them. Too often the training program does not build in such experimentation and practice. The problem with training meetings or

159

workshops away from the actual work situation is that there is no chance to try out new ways of behaving in the work situation. The hope is that people will have enough courage and insight to go back and try out a new behavior when it has never before been used in that setting. Thus, one of the hardest conditions to establish is allowing people the right to try out new things, to make mistakes, and to learn from them.

Climate

For a person to feel free to try out new things and to experiment with new behaviors and for others to give him feedback about how he is doing, there must be the right kind of climate in the situation. A person must feel free enough to try new things. If the climate is threatening and he feels he is being criticized or evaluated negatively or that anyone is going to laugh at him or mock him if he makes a mistake, he will probably feel most reluctant to change his behavior.

The optimum conditions discussed above seem most advantageous when combined in the immediate work setting. If conditions can be modified in the ongoing work situation to create the right kind of climate, if people can honestly look at their own performance, then if someone — a coach or consultant — can give them new ideas or directions, and if the conditions continue to be safe, it may be possible for a person to try out new ways of behaving that have a chance to continue.

Follow-up

Once a program of improvement is started, it needs to be continued. A follow-up on the change process is important. The follow-up program essentially means a repeat of the training conditions. Periodically the person in training needs to examine his performance, receive more feedback and data, gain new information, and then try again and again. If this process can be started and be built into the work activities of each person, it is possible to create a situation where every person is constantly working on his own improvement.

Organization Support

Too often training programs fail because the person returning to his job after a training program is not supported in new activities suggested by the training. New behavior, programs, and actions need to be encouraged and supported by one's superiors, peers, and subordinates. Team training (the training of a total work unit) is one way to help ensure that training is utilized in the organization. If one's superior supports the program of training, he can lend organizational support by rewarding the new behaviors through the regular organization channels.

It also improves the reinforcement of the new behaviors if the reward system supports the new actions immediately and directly.

References

Bradford, Leland, Jack Gibb, and Kenneth Benne
   1964   *T-Group Theory and Laboratory Method.* New York: John Wiley & Sons.

Dyer, William G.
   1972   *Modern Theory and Method in Group Training.* New York: Van Nostrand Reinhold Co.

Pfeiffer, William, and John Jones
   1969–74 *Structured Experiences for Human Relations Training,* vols. 1–5. Iowa City: University Associated Press.

Schein, Edgar, and Warren Bennis
   1965   *Personal and Organizational Changes Through Group Methods.* New York: John Wiley & Sons.

CONSULTING

Consulting with organizations regarding their improvement is a relatively new professional activity. There are two types of consultants: "outsiders," who come into the organization for a specified period and then leave, and "insiders," who are employed by the organization to work full time as consultants. Although there are some important differences between these roles, the results they are working for and the methods used are very similar.

All consultants need both to build a relationship with their "client" and to help the client plan for changes. These two activities — building a relationship and working for change — go on at all phases of the consulting process.

Much has been written about the role of the change agent, particularly from a theoretical point of view; however, the ongoing specifics of the change agent working in an organization have not been as clearly set forth. This chapter is an attempt to show the step-by-step actions I used as a consultant with an organization to bring about improvement.

Phase 1. Initial Contact

In this particular situation, I was contacted by two members of a government agency who held positions in the training, personnel, and public relations areas. The director of training and the director of public relations came to me and told me they were interested in establishing a development program for top management in their agency. They asked if I would be interested in such a program.

Question 1. The first question that I had to ask and answer for myself and the client was "Am I capable of providing the kind of resource this particular client needs?"

With this question in mind I told the two directors that I would be interested in working with such a training program only if the training the agency management needed was the type I was equipped to supply. This was agreeable to them, but they asked the next question.

Question 2. How can we determine just what training or development experience the management or client needs?

This is not an easy question, for there are at least these possibilities:

1. There may be some objective needs of that agency that could be determined by an outside, impartial analysis of the total functioning of the agency.

2. There may be needs of the management personnel that they feel subjectively but that may not be what is "objectively needed."

3. It is also possible that the subjective and objective needs are fairly close together.

Phase 2. The Contract

Following the initial contact, the consultant establishes a "contract" with the client. The contract can be formalized and written but is also always psychological: it is a set of expectations and understandings as to how the consultant will work. This contract may need to be reexamined and reformulated from time to time as the situation with the client changes.

In terms of dealing with this issue I made the following arrangement, which constituted the basic contract or agreement between us, with the people who contacted me: I would enter into a data-gathering process by interviewing all the top management who would normally be involved in a development program. I would try to be as objective as possible in gathering the information. I would tabulate and analyze the data to see what these men felt were their needs and the needs of the agency for development. I would present the data to them and on the basis of this information determine if the kind of resource I could supply would be compatible with the needs so uncovered.

I indicated immediately to them that if the problems of the agency were in such areas as fiscal, budgeting, state-federal relations, aspects of technical planning, and programming peculiar to the work of that agency, then I would not be a good resource. Using the Mann (1965) model — that the person in management needs a combination of technical, interpersonal, and cognitive skills — I indicated that if

163

their management felt they needed technical training or they needed to have a perspective about the total functioning of their agency and its programs, I would not be a good resource. If, however, their needs were in the area of interpersonal behavior — a lack of competence in dealing with human problems — then I felt I could be of assistance to them.

Phase 3. Data Collection: Entry and Relationship Development

From a strictly objective, scientific point of view, the collection of data should have been conducted by someone who would not be involved in the programs. It is possible that I, the consultant, could bias the data in directions I desired, particularly when there is a possibility of gain for me. While this method was desirable, it was not used. Trained personnel for collecting such data were not readily available. The work needed to be done immediately in light of time and budget requirements.

I made the decision to collect the data myself because I felt I could competently interview and analyze the data. I felt I could be objective within a suitable level. I did not personally "need" the contract from a financial point of view because my livelihood was not dependent on having or not having this contract.

Question 3. How can I become acquainted with the management personnel in such a way as to build a level of trust and confidence and obtain the information necessary to plan an effective future program?

I knew that my initial contact with the persons would be critical in terms of establishing a basis for an ongoing relationship. I therefore resolved to completely level with each person and to explain exactly my position and what I was trying to do.

Appointments were set up for me by the training officer, and I began the interviews. With each manager I explained: I was not hired to do a total development program. I was only trying to find out what they felt were their needs and those of the agency. In this way I would be able to make an assessment of the kind of program, if any, that was needed for improving their functioning and that of the agency.

Interview Questions

I used the following questions as a general guide in each interview:

   a. What is your job in the agency? Would you describe it to me?
   b. What do you think are the biggest problems you face in

doing your job?

c. What do you think you need personally in the way of training to improve your functioning in your job?

d. What do you think are the biggest problems facing the agency?

e. What do you think would help the agency to function better?

These were the general questions. I felt free to question further within the areas developed by the initial questions. Each interview lasted about two hours.

In addition to the interview data I also spent considerable time with the training director getting a picture of the agency organization, its programs, policies, and procedures. I also had available to me an employee attitude survey taken some eight years earlier. Besides this information, I read the agency handbook and other literature describing its work.

From the interviews I tabulated the data by problems or needs mentioned in the interviews. I listed all items of concern mentioned by three or more people and put them on newsprint.

Phase 4. Decision for Further Action

A meeting was then called of all top-level managers. At this meeting I presented the list of problems or concerns. I pointed out those problems in the agency that I felt I could help and those that were not in my area of competency. I listed for them all of the general areas of their concerns that I felt were within my resource capacity to help, such as these:

1. Dealing with conflict
2. Improving communications and feedback
3. Improving staff meetings and the procedures for planning
4. Improving the decision-making process
5. Widening the base of acceptance in the management staff
6. Improving motivation

During the meeting I was concerned with the next question:

Question 4. If I work with this staff, how can I develop a relationship where they are committed to investing themselves in a program of training and development?

I felt that if this group were to have a program of development and if they were to develop any commitment to the program, they would have to decide if they wanted me to work with them. I told them, following the data presentation, they should decide whether they wanted to follow a program in the areas of my competence.

Further, I indicated that I did not want the agency director, the training director, or others to put pressures on them to go ahead with this. It should be the consent of each person to participate or not in such a program, if it were accepted. Following these remarks I left the room, telling them that I would like them to make a decision and inform me at my home later. I tried to assure them that they should do what they felt was best for the agency — not make a decision to please me or anyone else. With that I left and returned home. The next day I was contacted by the training officer, who reported that after an hour's discussion the program was unanimously accepted and that all could participate.

Phase 5. The Development Program

At the decision-making meeting I had outlined a proposed development program within my areas of competence so the group would have some basis for making a decision about participating in the program. I felt it was not fair to ask them to decide for or against a program without some indication as to what the program would be like. The proposed program was as follows:

Proposed Management and Organization Development Program

I. Initial Three-Day Laboratory
   A. The purpose of this intensive period is to provide an opportunity for participants and the consultant to create a situation where all may examine and begin to work on the following:
      1. The level of acceptance in management
      2. Level of communication in the staff
      3. Decision-making procedures in the staff
      4. Areas of conflict among staff members
      5. The interpersonal competence level and management style of each staff member
   B. At the laboratory certain new concepts of organization and management would be introduced.
II. Follow-up Consultation
   Following the laboratory, the consultant would meet with each participant to review with him the findings of the laboratory period and to help him plan a program for his own improvement and the improvement of his department.
III. Short Seminars
   In addition to the follow-up consultations, some seminar periods would be held to talk about problems of organization and management.

Laboratory Design

FIRST DAY

- General orientation
- Group problem-solving exercise. Ranking effective managerial characteristics. Group observation, with process analysis.
- Discussion and summary
- Lunch
- Group problem-solving exercise
- Discussion and summary

SECOND DAY

- Lecture: Management style
- Group discussion: Each manager describes his own management style, how he feels he functions, and his assessments of his own strengths and weaknesses.
- Lunch
- Continuation of group discussion

THIRD DAY

- Feedback to managers. Each manager who would like feedback about how others see his performance in the agency may request to receive feedback from the group.
- Continuation of feedback through the day
- Concluding dinner

Question 5. What kind of training program can be developed to involve the staff members at a significant level so learning can begin?

In discussions with the agency administrator and the training director, it was suggested that T-group or sensitivity group training was somewhat suspect among some of the management staff, and it was recommended that this format not be used. They were referring particularly to the completely unstructured T-group situation, which was not thought to help focus on the problems of the organization. I agreed not to have the completely unstructured situation and to center the three-day program on matters of concern to the staff members.

The above design allowed me to examine with the group most of the problem areas that fell within my realm of concern. The first day was a relatively structured day — and nonthreatening. It allowed me to further build a relationship with the staff and to watch them work together on some imposed problems. The laboratory allowed us to examine the nature of problem solving, planning, decision making, conflict areas within the staff, level of acceptance of staff members, and to open channels of communication and feedback to various staff members.

Phase 6. The Follow-up Program

Question 6. What type of follow-up activity will help implement the gains of the laboratory in the back-home situation?

By its very nature, a laboratory program conducted in-house with people who have ongoing relationships has certain advantages. Any improvements in relationships gained in the program have great possibilities for continuing. However, I felt that each manager needed to have an opportunity to review the feedback given him during the laboratory and to have help in planning a program of improvement based on this new information.

During the discussion of management style and the feedback sessions that followed, I took extensive notes on each person. I had a complete description of his self-perception and also the feedback of the staff about him. Within a month after the laboratory, I began another series of consultation interviews with each participant.

In these sessions I reviewed with each manager what he had said about himself and then what others had shared with him in the way of feedback about his performance. This information was discussed at length and I asked each man, "In light of this information, what do you think you should be doing to improve your performance?" I then tried to help each person think through a concrete plan for improvement based on the feedback given.

Of critical importance were the sessions spent with the top men in the agency, the administrator and assistant administrator. Both of these men accepted the development program and openly supported all activities. A great deal of feedback was given in the sessions to both of them, and both developed concrete plans to improve. Support from the top levels seemed to encourage others to give and receive feedback more openly and to plan for change with some optimism that change could be effected.

Phase 7. Termination

Question 7. How can I leave the client functioning effectively after my role as consultant has ended?

In the consulting program it is important that the relationship with the client system be terminated at a point where the client system has developed enough independence to continue a program of improvement without the consultant.

Termination was not considered until each manager had a concrete plan for his own improvement, an intermediate progress report had been circulated from the consultant to the total staff on what had been happening in the development program thus far, and then a final writen report given to all, outlining the program, the gains made, and the work still to be done as seen by the consultant.

A formal termination session was then held. The final report was reviewed and discussed, followed by a closing dinner.

Discussion — Apparent Gains of the Program

Missing in this training program is an evaluation of the program. This needs to be done, preferably by someone not connected with the training and at some time period following the training program. Unfortunately, too few organizations have budget and program policies that build in evaluation of programs. Thus any evaluation of the program at this point can be only very subjective at best.

On the basis of my follow-up interviews with each manager, certain gains were commonly mentioned to me as being apparent to them:

1. The administrator had gained a new insight into methods of decision making. He was making a real attempt in staff meetings to arrive at consensus for decisions that affected the total agency or consensus among those who would be affected by the decision.

2. Persons with differences explored in the feedback sessions had gone to each other and continued to work on ways of resolving differences.

3. Some persons had made some direct behavior changes, such as getting out of the office more and visiting others, consulting with others before making decisions, speaking up more in staff meetings,

taking more time to listen to subordinates.

4. Some persons had been able to clarify certain of their staff functions in the agency as a result of being able to talk about their roles.

5. Certain of the younger and newer members of the management staff felt greater acceptance and more ease in the staff group than before and as a result felt freer to contribute in the staff meetings.

References

Argyris, Chris
  1970   *Intervention Theory and Method.* Reading, Mass.: Addison-Wesley.

Mann, Floyd C.
  1965   Toward an understanding of the leadership role in formal organization. In R. Dubin, *Leadership and Productivity.* San Francisco: Chandler Publishing Co., 68–103.

Schein, Edgar, Warren Bennis, and Richard Beckhard
  1969   *Organization Development Series.* Reading, Mass.: Addison-Wesley.

Steele, Fritz
  1975   *Consulting for Organization Change.* Amherst: University of Massachusetts Press.

HELPING

According to most people, effectively working with other people requires that we first "build a good relationship." Other ways of stating this same axiom are "develop rapport," "establish a good climate," or "gain their confidence." Unfortunately most discussions stop at this point as though the subject were covered once the principle is stated. Each person is left to his own devices as to what should be done in establishing what is the critical base of the whole subsequent working relationship. Yet central to the work of any manager or change agent is working with others in ways that will allow work to be accomplished and changes achieved.

What is important in building this effective or "good" relationship? Fortunately some good research and theory can help develop an answer to this question.

Individual Needs

As the person who desires to be helpful contacts another person, he should keep in mind that this other person represents a collection of needs or conditions of the organism that demand some satisfaction, or if satisfaction is not practical, then some adjustment must be made. These needs have been described in many ways, and there is no final definitive cataloging of the need system. One useful model is that developed by Maslow (1943:370–96) who felt that there is a hierarchy of human needs, each need in the hierarchy dependent on those below it in the system. (See the discussion of Maslow in the chapter on motivation.)

While this conception of the human needs system may not be

171

entirely accurate or adequate, still it points out one important factor in building a relationship with others. If it is true that each person has a collection of personal needs, then it would seem that the person who would not meet these needs or who would even violate them would not build the same type of relationship as one who could meet them. Too often, in the interest of getting the job done, the concentration is on the task and not in taking into account the needs of the person. In building a helping relationship, it is especially important to take into account the social, ego, and self-actualizing needs of others.

Individual Values

Each person is not only a complex system of needs, but is also a system of values. Every person has a set of feelings about certain ideas, concepts, situations, or activities that represents points of concern, of worth, and of importance. Individual value systems vary, and what is valuable to one person may not be valuable to another. For example, say that Mr. Andrews values his privacy and his right to make his own decisions; he values the opinion of a certain newspaper columnist and the efficacy of prayer as a means of final answers to questions. Should a person come to be "helpful" with him and not know or try to understand his value system, the helpful person may engage in activities, make remarks, or suggest actions that are in direct opposition to what Mr. Andrews holds to be of value. Should this occur, the relationship would probably not be one of rapport or confidence; rather it would be strained, antagonistic, uncooperative, and perhaps even hostile. As in the case with human needs, the person desiring to build a good relationship would find it advantageous to understand the other person's value system and to respect it in the course of the interaction.

Individual Expectations

An individual's need system and value system are independent of the person desiring to build a relationship. They are rather constant factors continually in operation. However, another complex of attitudes is important in the building of an effective helping relationship. It consists of the expectations the client has of the helping person.

Expectations are the feelings one person has that another person should behave in certain ways. Sometimes expectations are shared: each person knows what others expect of him, and the result is one of cohesion and harmony as people meet each other's expectations and consequently reward each other. When expectations are not met, it is predicted that negative reactions, conflict, and disharmony will result. From this it would appear that if the change agent (CA) does not meet the expectations of the client or the system members, negative reactions would occur and the basic relationship would not be one of rapport, cohesion, or confidence.

It sometimes happens that one person will consciously and deliberately violate or fail to meet the expectations of another person, but this is an unusual occurrence. More likely is the probability that one person's failure to meet the expectations of another person results from a lack of information about the other's expectation system. To ensure a situation of nonviolation of expectations, the CA must know the expectations of the system member as well as the needs and values of the persons in the system (the client system).

The Change Agent's Role

If the above conceptions are valid and people do indeed have needs, values, and expectations that are important to them, it would follow that if one person behaves in ways that do not meet another's needs or that violate his values and expectations, the resulting relationship would not be conducive to working together effectively.

Basic to successful functioning within the boundaries of a person's needs, values, and expectations systems is understanding what these are. How does one go about finding out these important dimensions from another person?

Some guidelines for gaining this understanding follow:

Leveling

In opening the interaction with the client system, the CA may attempt to start the relationship on the basis that each participant will "level" with the other person. The attempt is to establish a basic ground rule that is fundamental to the whole relationship — namely, complete frankness and honesty with each other.

If the client system indicates a willingness to adopt such a ground rule, then the CA may wish to ask the members of the system to let him know honestly how they feel concerning their needs, values, and expectations. He might ask for information such as the following:

1. When is it most convenient for me to come and work with you? (What are your expectations about time arrangements?)

2. What do you think I ought to do when I work with you?

3. Do you have any apprehensions or feelings of anxiety about having me come?

4. How do you feel about the conditions you have in your system?

5. What bothers you most about your situation in this system?

Sharing

An important part of the leveling process is the reciprocal sharing of data between the CA and the individual. A good working relationship is based on mutual understanding and shared confidence. It is as important for the CA to level with the person as is the reverse. The CA is at something of a disadvantage in sharing ideas, information, and feelings with the person, for his professional role sometimes limits the amount of data he can share. However, the CA may talk with the system members about such things as:

1. What I see my role to be in working with you.
2. What I think a good CA-client relationship should be.
3. Some of the anxieties I have in performing my work.
4. What I see as some of my competencies in working with you.

The keynote is that both the CA and the individual *begin* their experience by talking about the relationship. The ultimate concern is the achievement of system objectives, but the relationship must be built in order to work effectively on the problems.

Individual Differences

It is a common cliché that "all people are different," but it is important to keep this fact in mind. The individual mix of needs, values, and expectations is going to be different for every person. No one approach will handle every situation. The CA needs to develop or increase his sensitivity. *Sensitivity* has been defined as the ability to discriminate clearly among individuals on the basis of their characteristics. Some persons are capable of seeing individual differences more accurately than others and are thus able to respond more appropriately. Dubin summarizes this way, "The more successful supervisor may be the one best able to perceive these individual characteristics in order to tailor his own actions to the individual's unique qualities" (1965:39).

If the ability to differentiate between individuals and to respond appropriately to these differences is an important aspect of the CA-client relationship, increasing this ability would be an important part of the training of persons who must work closely with others. If it is possible to teach people to be more perceptive and sensitive to others, this training should be part of the program of education for CAs. Persons who are rather rigid and inflexible in their responses to others may have difficulty in making the appropriate modifications for individual differences. Perhaps this inflexibility, if it cannot be modified, should be an important consideration in the selection of CAs, whose jobs put them into contact with many different people. Certainly there is some research evidence that sensitivity and flexibility are important in good interpersonal relations, and the question now is *how* to increase these behaviors in the CA.

The Communication of Acceptance

From the fields of counseling and therapy comes the notion of interpersonal acceptance. This involves the subtle communication from one person to another of genuine interest and concern and, more importantly, willingness to try to understand the other person exactly the way he is, without evaluation and judgment.

Feelings of nonacceptance can be communicated in many ways, both verbally and nonverbally. A common experience of persons working in homes of those in a social-class level different from their own is a sense of revulsion toward people living in conditions so unlike what they are used to. If a person working with a lower-class family were to react negatively to the unsanitary surroundings, so as to imply, "You're dirty and I'm not. I'm better than you are," one would predict that a feeling of nonacceptance would be established.

Nonacceptance and Acceptance

What are the behaviors that tend to make a person feel accepted or nonaccepted? The diagram on page 176 may help identify behavioral inputs that result in feelings of acceptance or nonacceptance.

What are the results of the nonaccepting relationship? It would be predicted that if the system member did not honestly feel acceptance from the CA, some of the following things might occur:

1. *Results of nonacceptance*
   a. Antagonistic feelings
   b. Noncooperation
   c. Avoidance of the person
   d. Little sharing of information
   e. Noncompliance with suggestions or advice
   f. Feelings of relief when the relationship is terminated

All the above are conditions that would plague the CA and prevent him from accomplishing his goals with the system. On the other hand, if the CA were able to develop the kind of accepting relationship discussed here, we would predict more of the following:

2. *Results of acceptance*
   a. Sharing of information
   b. Cooperation
   c. Feelings of closeness
   d. Willingness to work interdependently
   e. Welcome and anticipation of one's return

Problems in Developing a Helping Relationship

As indicated above, the behavioral inputs from the CA to the system influence the feelings of acceptance or nonacceptance. One

Behavioral Inputs

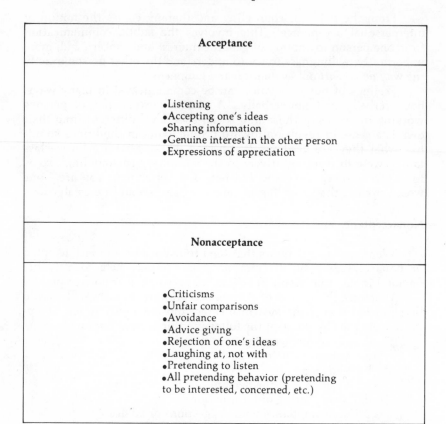

Acceptance
•Listening •Accepting one's ideas •Sharing information •Genuine interest in the other person •Expressions of appreciation
Nonacceptance
•Criticisms •Unfair comparisons •Avoidance •Advice giving •Rejection of one's ideas •Laughing at, not with •Pretending to listen •All pretending behavior (pretending to be interested, concerned, etc.)

of the real problems for the CA is to get a clear picture of how his behavior is being experienced by the system members he is trying to help. If the CA thinks his behavioral inputs are appropriate, he will continue to behave in the same way until he discovers they are not. Some ways of checking one's behavioral inputs include —

1. An evaluation questionnaire circulated to the system members.

2. Periodic interviews by supervisors or an outside person to check on the reaction of system members.

3. A visit to the system by an observer who could watch the CA in action. (Following this, an honest exchange of information would be given.)

4. Tape-recording a visit, with subsequent critique by a group of colleagues. (The important thing is to get an honest evaluation of performance as the work with others progresses.)

It is apparent that building an effective relationship involves not only information about what is needed but also skills in working with others and attitudes appropriate to the goal. In this respect, training persons to build effective relationships with others requires a concentration on information, skills, and attitudes. Too much current learning emphasis is based primarily on the acquiring of information.

References

Benjamin, Alfred
   1969   *The Helping Interview*, New York: Houghton Mifflin Co.

Dubin, Robert
   1965   *Leadership and Productivity.* San Francisco: Chandler Publishing Company: 39.

Fordyce, Jack, and Raymond Weil
   1971   *Managing with People.* Reading, Mass.: Addison-Wesley.

Maslow, Abraham H.
   1943   A theory of human motivation. *Psychological Review* 50:370–96.

GROUP TRAINER*

The group is the vehicle for many training and development programs, and the development of skills for working with groups is an important area for a person concerned with changes. Central in the whole area of human-relations training with emphasis on the training group (and to an important degree in discussion groups, group-centered classroom situations, and group counseling or therapy) is the trainer. While some training programs have eliminated the trainer, in most others he still represents an important element in the total learning environment (Blake and Mouton, 1962:61–77).

To those involved in conducting training groups certain key questions have been presented concerning the behavior of the trainer, or educator, as Argyris (1962:153) prefers. Some questions have been these:

1. How active should I be in participating in the group?

2. What kinds of things should I do when I intervene in the activities of the group?

3. What kind of relationship should I establish with the group members — should I stay aloof or become one of the group?

It is with the second of these questions that this chapter is concerned: What are the types of interventions open to a trainer as he conducts his group, and what are the probable implications and consequences of these various types of interventions? It is hoped that this inventory of interventions may allow more systematic analysis of trainer behavior and its resulting effects. An intervention is any action taken in an effort to influence the activities of group members.

*Revised. Reprinted by special permission from *Human Relations Training News.* William G. Dyer, "An inventory of trainer interventions," 7 (Spring 1963).

Types of Interventions

Focusing on Content

In content focus the trainer actually comments on or contributes to the topic of discussion. If, for example, the group is discussing the topic "How should an effective supervisor behave?" the trainer might share an experience, some research data, or his opinion concerning the topic at hand.

Comment: Since the behavior of the trainer is often seen as a model for group members to follow, a content intervention may give legitimacy to the topic and perpetuate its discussion. If, however, as is usually the case, the focus is on what is happening in the group "here and now," a content intervention may keep the group from looking at its own processes. Where the focus is on content, content intervention may contribute to the goals of the group, providing the trainer does not make a contribution another group member might make.

Focusing on Process

Process focus attempts to direct the attention to what is happening in the group "here and now." One standard intervention (almost to the point of becoming a cliché among trainers) is for the trainer to say, "I wonder what is really going on in the group now," or "Why are we doing this?" Another common intervention might be to focus on process by pointing out a process condition, such as "Were you all aware that only two persons voiced an opinion, yet a decision was made?"

Comment: There are a wide variety of ways a trainer may help the group focus on its own processes. The ways actually selected by the trainer are probably determined by his own personal style or by his explicit or implicit strategy for bringing about the learnings he desires to develop. Argyris (1962:166–67) has this to say about the process intervention that begins with "I wonder": "I would not [use this phrasing] because this would be dishonest. I am really *not* wondering. I believe I know why they are doing it. And perhaps more important, I believe they feel that I know. Dishonesty does not lead to authentic relationships."

Asking for Feelings

The trainer may want to attempt to draw data from group members as to how they feel about certain conditions or situations that have occurred in the group. An intervention of this type would be "Ed, how did you feel when the group rejected your idea?" This is really a type of process intervention, for it often leads to a looking at what has happened. In addition it solicits member reactions to what has happened.

179

Comment: Some trainers and many participants find the sharing of feelings the most interesting part of the training process. For some, it is the first time they have been able to find out how others feel about how they behave. Certainly this is an important and legitimate learning goal. However, if the trainer concentrates on this type of intervention, he may neglect a number of other important facets of group action. The matter of focus on feeling versus group variables has been an important issue in human relations training (Bradford, Benne, and Gibb, 1964).

Giving Direction

At times the trainer may intervene to give the group certain suggestions, directions, procedures, or ground rules which influence the direction the group takes. Early in the group's life the trainer may structure activity by having members write out name cards, use a tape recorder, or stop at some given time. At other times, he may provide observation forms, suggest they use a group observer, try out an exercise, or role play.

Comment: Trainers differ in their use of direction-giving interventions. Some offer direction only in the form of suggestions, and others, by virtue of their status position, arbitrarily impose certain actions on group members. Both positions have a rationale: those preferring suggestions feel group members should be the ones to make their own decisions, and those favoring an imposed direction feel group members should have the experience of dealing with this type of behavior and learn to cope with such forced direction — especially if they dislike it.

If a trainer has great need to control, he may intervene often with direction giving, or he may recognize this need in himself and overreact, not supplying direction to the group when it would be helpful. A critical point in training often comes when the group is floundering and not learning. The trainer must then decide either to let the group try to work through its own impasse or to supply some direction. A decision must be reached after considering the dilemma of perhaps reinforcing dependency or, on the other hand, permitting the group to waste time and wallow in frustration beyond what is desirable for learning. In such situations, the trainer must think about such factors as the length of the training program, his judgment as to the level of dependency, the resources available to the group, and his own tolerance for ambiguity.

Giving Direct Feedback

At certain times the trainer may intervene by giving direct feedback to a member or to the group as a whole. When and how this is done again depends on the strategy of the trainer.

Comment: Some trainers prefer to give direct feedback early in the life of the group, both as a model to group members and to legitimize this type of response. Others prefer to wait until they have worked through some of the authority problems with group members, fearing the effects of feedback from the trainer until the authority issue has been dealt with. Here again the trainer is faced with a dilemma. Group members are often anxious, and properly so, to know how the trainer, really the only trained person in the group, sees the group and the individual members. The reactions of the trainer, however, are often no more valid or important than feedback from other group members. The trainer must somehow share his feedback and at the same time get the group to gather and appreciate the feedback data of all its members.

Feedback to the group involves the expression of the trainer's reactions to what has been going on in the group. The same issues involved in expressing feedback to individuals are connected with giving group feedback.

Providing Cognitive Orientations

Occasionally the trainer may feel it important to give some general theory or information elaborating or clarifying or providing insight into an experience the group has had. Some may give a "lecturette," or others may talk briefly with the group.

Comment: The trainer must face the question "If I take time to provide the insight, will it heighten the learning process, or will the participants learn more if they can glean the same insight from their own experiences?" The trainer must be careful that he does not monopolize the time by giving a great deal of cognitive information (perhaps satisfying his own need to be seen as an expert) but really minimizing the benefit that comes from letting people learn for themselves.

Performing Group Task-maintenance Functions

According to Benne and Sheats (1948:42–47), there is a series of various task and maintenance activities that should be performed if a group is going to accomplish its task and maintain itself as an effective human system. Assuming the task of the training group is to facilitate the learnings of the participants, the trainer often intervenes and performs a number of the task-maintenance functions necessary to promote learning.

Task functions include the following (these and the list of maintenance functions are taken largely from Benne and Sheats [1948]):

1. *Opinion seeking.* The trainer asks group members for their reactions to what has happened in the group.

2. *Opinion giving.* The trainer shares his opinion as to what he thinks is going on in the group.

3. *Initiating.* Initiating is similar to direction giving mentioned above. The authors say of this role, "[It] may take the form of suggestions of a new group goal or a new definition of the problem. It may take the form of a suggested solution or some way of handling a difficulty that the group has encountered. Or it may take the form of a proposed new procedure for the group, a new way of organizing the group for the task ahead" (Benne and Sheats, 1948:44).

4. *Elaborating.* The trainer expands or develops an idea already presented by others.

5. *Coordinating.* The trainer tries to pull together different ideas or suggestions already introduced into the group.

6. *Summarizing.* The trainer summarizes what he feels has been going on in the group or what he feels have been some of the important insights gained.

7. *Consensus testing.* The trainer asks group members if they were all in agreement concerning a certain decision or action effected in the group.

8. Performing technical procedures. The person performing technical functions "expedites group movement by doing things for the group — performing routine tasks, e.g., distributing materials, or manipulating objects for the group, rearranging the seating or running the recording machine, etc." (Benne and Sheats, 1948:44). This represents something of a physical intervention in the group.

9. Reality testing. When it has been suggested by the group that a member, or the group, behave in a certain way or try out certain actions, the trainer intervenes and helps members explore whether this action is really possible or desirable.

Maintenance functions include the following:

1. Encouraging. The trainer intervenes by praising, supporting, or otherwise accepting the contributions of group members.

2. Harmonizing. The trainer intervenes by trying to reconcile differences that occur between group members.

3. Gate keeping. The trainer encourages or facilitates participation by group members.

4. Standard setting. The trainer expresses a standard or norm he feels would help the group reach its learning goals (Bradford, Benne, and Gibb, 1964).

Classifying Individual Roles

Benne and Sheats (1948:42–47) mention that sometimes individuals use the group to satisfy individual needs and perform certain actions. They classify such persons as aggressors, blockers, recognition seekers, self-confessors, playboys, or dominators. Trainers may intervene at times in this manner, but it is questionable whether these types of interventions facilitate the learnings of group members.

Comment: When and how often the trainer performs various task-maintenance functions for the group depends on his strategy. Some will intervene extensively early in training task-maintenance functions, not only to provide a model for group participants, but also to get certain important things done. Since group members have not yet developed an understanding of these functions or the ability to perform them, the trainer supplies them as he sees they are needed. As members develop greater ability to perform these group functions, the trainer may reduce his own efforts. Then, when certain functions are needed, the trainer may intervene to focus on process and to ask why certain functions have not been performed in the group.

Diagnosing

From time to time the trainer may present to the group his diagnosis of what he sees happening in the group. He may do this by suggesting a hypothesis or series of hypotheses as to what has contributed to the situation or condition he observes. For example, group members may recognize apathy among themselves and be at a loss to understand or explain it. The trainer may intervene with a diagnosis of the situation something like this: "There are a number of possibilities why the group is apathetic. One hypothesis is that our goals are either not clear or are too broad. Another hypothesis is that we are afraid if we start to work again old conflicts may be reopened." He may then ask for other possibilities from group members or suggest that they examine their own reactions to the forces connected with the apathetic condition. His intervention is part of his strategy to get the group to enter into a process of diagnosing group problems.

Comment: Diagnostic intervention is somewhere between opinion giving and developing a level of theory or insight (cognitive orientation). It is an exploratory, suggesting, hypothesizing type of comment. Its purpose is to suggest ways of looking at and trying to understand what has been happening in the group.

Protecting Group Members

Another type of intervention has been suggested by Blake (Bradford, Benne, and Gibb, 1964), who feels the trainer should intervene at certain points to protect certain individual members. This type of intervention may or may not be in the repertoire of the trainer, depending on his theory of training. The intervention calls for the trainer to keep members from "overexposing" their behavior, that is, sharing personal incidents, feelings, reactions that may not be appropriate to the goals of the group. Overexposure of behavior may create a group situation with which neither the members nor the trainer is capable of dealing.

A trainer may also feel a need to protect a group member if he feels that feedback to the person is ill timed or unnecessarily severe. Or it may be necessary to protect the individuality of a member, to allow him to maintain his own identity despite certain group pressures to conform.

Comment: Some trainers would not use this intervention but would, when a situation arose calling for protection, focus on the process and ask the group if the behavior in which they were engaging was really appropriate to the goals. A direct protection intervention would call for the trainer to say, "Joe, I think you are going too far at this point." It may really be only a special type of feedback intervention.

Interventions and Strategy

A trainer's intervention is only part of his total strategy, or his overall plan for bringing about the learning goals he has established. It involves such factors as:

1. Timing — when and how often does he intervene?
2. Issues — around what concerns does he intervene?

3. Emotion — how much of his own emotional makeup and reactions are funneled into the group (his use of humor, anger, praise, warmth)?

4. Structure — how much control and direction does he maintain over the group?

5. Interpersonal relations — what is his relationship with group members? Does he try to become a group member, maintain his trainer status uniquely, participate with group members outside the group?

6. Theory of individual and group behavior — his own orientation concerning individual and group dynamics will determine in part what he "sees" going on, around what concerns he will try to focus, and what learnings he will emphasize.

One of the difficult questions in training is "What strategy or strategies are the most effective in bringing about the desired learnings?" Thus far, little attempt has been made to answer this question objectively. At this point, at least, training is much more an art than a science. While it may never be possible or desirable to reduce training to a standardized set of responses, still, if more trainers are to be developed and training improved, there must be some attempts to ascertain what type of trainer style or strategy produces maximum learning.

One way to objectify training for research and analysis purposes is to observe and catalog systematically the trainer's intervention along the lines mentioned above to see what pattern of intervention maximizes certain measured learning goals.

Interventions and the Trainer

In an interesting study, Reisel (1962:93–108) pointed out some important effects the trainer's personality has on the types of interventions he makes. Reisel shows that in addition to the strategy the trainer holds, either explicitly or implicitly, there are certain forces within him that influence his training behavior. The trainer will intervene in terms of his own needs to control, to be accepted and liked, and to succeed. He has his own peculiar patterns of responding to anxiety, conflict, and ambiguity. He may not be at all aware of how these internal forces influence his behavior in the training process.

In addition to these more deep-seated dimensions, the trainer also has language and speech patterns, physical mannerisms, and gestures that become part of his intervention. Thus the type of intervention — how it is used in his strategy — plus certain personality traits of his own combine to influence the effect of his intervention.

An intervention inventory may bring to light some of the factors in the trainer's personality that influence training. One would hypothesize that the trainer with high needs to control might use more direction giving, cognitive orientation, direct feedback, and summarizing interventions. The trainer who avoids conflicts and feelings may find it more comfortable to make content and direction interventions and to perform harmonizing functions when conflict occurs.

Summary

An important part of the current training process is the influence of the trainer on the training group. Since the trainer's primary effect is through the interventions he makes in the course of the group's activities, it may be valuable to study more systematically the nature of these interventions, how they are used, and their subsequent effect. This is an attempt to catalog these interventions with some suggestions as to how this inventory might be utilized in further research on the role of the trainer.

References

Argyris, Chris
   1962   *Interpersonal Competence and Organizational Effectiveness.* Homewood, Ill.: Irwin-Dorsey Press, 153, 166–67.

Benne, Kenneth D., and P. Sheats
   1948   Functional roles of group members. *Journal of Social Issues* 4 (Spring): 42–47.

Blake, Robert R., and Jane S. Mouton
   1962   The instrumental training laboratory. In *Issues in Training.* Washington: National Training Laboratories, 61–77.

Bradford, Leland P., Kenneth D. Benne, and Jack R. Gibb (eds.)
   1964   *T-Group Theory and Laboratory Method.* New York: Wiley and Sons.

Dyer, William G.
   1972   *Modern Theory and Method in Group Training.* New York: Van Nostrand Reinhold.

Reisel, Jerry
   1962   Observations on the trainer role: A case study. *Leadership and Organization: A Behavioral Approach.* New York: McGraw-Hill. Reprinted in *Issues in Training.* Washington: National Training Laboratories, 93–108.

FAMILY UNITS

Not all consulting and change efforts are made within the context of large-scale business or government organizations. Sometimes the focus is on the small unit, the place where people live in the most fundamental sense. Sometimes this basic unit is the real family — parents and children. At other times the person working with change is involved with a tight-knit work group, social group, club, neighborhood, or organization similar to a family. The issue for the change agent is "How do I work with this total system? All members are going to be affected if the behavior of one changes!" It takes skill to move into this family system and create conditions in which all family members are involved and supportive of the change efforts.

Helping Family-type Units

How does a person help a family-type unit? Too often the one who comes into a family situation is seen as the expert, and reaction to an expert can be either one of hostility and suspicion or one of overwhelming acceptance with an accompanying dependency on the expert to handle all the problems.

How does the change agent (CA) deal with the matter of dependency on him? Here the CA must have some insights about himself. One of the ways of handling dependency is to encourage it. This strategy would be characteristic of a person who finds great satisfaction in having persons dependent on him. Dependency can be flattering. Some research has indicated that people can in many ways encourage others to be dependent and at the same time deny they are doing any such thing.

187

Another possible strategy for dealing with dependency is to reject the dependent person — hold him at arm's length, refuse to enter into any type of close relationship that would foster or support any dependency at all. This process may eliminate dependency but may also lead to two equally uncomfortable consequences: (1) a situation of counterdependency may occur where the person with the problem is rebellious, negative, and resistant to anything the CA has to offer, or (2) a sense of apathy, isolation, or noninvolvement between the person and the CA, where the person remains aloof, feeling that the CA does not really want to understand him or accept him and does not really want to help him.

The problem is this: How can the CA build an accepting, supportive, helping relationship with members of the family without building such a dependency relationship that he cannot finally leave them to function independently?

Parsons and Fox (1958) suggest two behaviors that are important in this connection. One, the helping person will adhere scrupulously to a professional attitude, that is, respond consistently as an interested, concerned professional and not be trapped into behaving in ways that are not consistent with professional conduct. Two, the person who is helping the one with the problem introduces conditional rewards, particularly approving the person for gaining insight into his own situation and behavior. These responses are consistent with general practices according to some therapeutic models.

Gibb's Trust Model

Jack R. Gibb (Bradford, Benne, and Gibb, 1964: 679–710) has suggested another model for looking at the sequential steps that lead finally to a situation where a person functions in a mature way, being neither dependent nor counterdependent but appropriately interdependent. That is, he is capable of accepting help when it is appropriate and moving ahead on his own when that is called for.

The final condition of mature self-control is based on successfully achieving the conditions specified at the prior three levels. The basic underpinning of the whole developmental sequence is a condition of basic understanding and trust; hence the term *trust model* has been applied to Gibb's formulation.

Each condition is dependent on the prior condition, so this suggests the sequence of problems, actions, and behaviors with which the CA must deal in working with others. Our concern here is to apply this model to the area of the CA-family relationship and see what implications this model has for the training and functioning of CAs, particularly those who must deal with the family in the home setting. As has been earlier pointed out, the home setting is probably the most difficult setting for achieving the end result of self-control.

Trust Model

STEP 1
Basic Conditions
Acceptance or Trust

Desired Consequences	**Deviant Consequences**
Acceptance and trust of others, understanding, empathy	Distrust of others, fear, resistance, suspicion

STEP 2
Basic Conditions
Data Flow

Desired Consequences	**Deviant Consequences**
Open, two-way communications, with wide sharing of important, sensitive information	Closed, restricted, one-way communications, little sharing of real feelings or sensitive information

STEP 3
Basic Conditions
Goal Setting and Decision Making

Desired Consequences	**Deviant Consequences**
Person sets own goals, participates in making decisions	Goals set by others, decisions made by others

STEP 4
Basic Conditions
Control

Desired Consequences	**Deviant Consequences**
Self-control, interdependence	Imposed control, checking up on, following around, threatening

Let us take each condition in sequence and look at its implications for the helping person.

Acceptance and Trust

According to this model, the initial basic concern that people have as they encounter each other (in the case in point, when the person first faces the CA) is "Who is this person, what does he want, what is he going to try to do to me?" People wonder, "Can I trust him? Will he tell me the truth? Should I tell him everything? Will he really help me? Will he understand how I feel?" Somehow the CA must anticipate these concerns and deal with them successfully. Gibb in his research found that in the area of trust the law of reciprocity seems to operate. That is, people tend to respond in kind, and when they are treated with acceptance and are trusted, they tend to accept and trust in return.

Almost all new CAs facing their first experience in this field are counseled by their instructors to learn to *accept the people they visit in the conditions as they find them.* The CA should accept people in their environment. He must work in the home; he cannot accept the person only if he is clean, neat, polite, and obedient. He does not need to accept the conditions of the home in the sense that he must agree with them or like them, but he must learn to accept the person he visits in the home.

The visiting CA must communicate to the person and his family, for he is working now with the total family, not just with the person with a problem. "I think I understand how you feel since I am trained to understand problems. I think I can help you; at least I want to try. I will try to be perfectly honest with you, and I will level with you at all times. I will keep my word with you. I will keep your confidences. I will not make fun of you or laugh at you." Something of this nature appears to be at the root of an honest, trusting relationship. The CA says in effect, "I do not think ill of you for having this problem. I do not look down on you, nor do I think that I am better than you are. I think you are a worthwhile person and that you have capabilities for handling your own situation."

If the CA himself can be accepting and trustworthy, then the prediction is that the family in turn will respond in the same way. It is difficult, if not impossible, to make others accept or trust you. It would appear that people trust as they are trusted and accept others as they are accepted.

A trusting relationship is not built all at once. It seems that the level of trust is continually being tested, and it continues to grow or to diminish as we work at the other conditions. The CA works at his task of treating the problem conditions, and while he works he builds the relationship with the family. These two vital activities are going on simultaneously. He must work at them both together.

190

Data Flow

The amount of information that is shared between the CA and the family is a function of the level of trust that has been established, according to Gibb's trust model. If the CA sees the person and the family as being stupid, unfriendly, uncooperative, disinterested, and uninformed, then he is not likely to share very much information with them. The reverse is also true. If the family members see the CA as unconcerned, unfriendly, unaccepting, and not trustworthy, then they will probably tell him very little of how they really feel, what their real concerns and problems are. One CA was heard to say, "How can I get people to tell me the truth? I ask them questions about their activities, and I know they are lying to me." One would predict that the trust between the CA and the family is not at an adequate level. It would appear that the individual or the family feels that if they tell the CA the truth he will punish them in some way or think poorly of them or "bawl" them out. When people hold back information or distort the data, it is usually because they are not confident and secure in their relationships with the persons with whom they are communicating.

CAs are caught in a dilemma in the area of sharing data, for here it seems that openness begets openness of communications. CAs often feel they cannot tell all they know or suspect, for they fear they will lose contact with the family if they say too much. Indeed, all CAs are aware of situations where the CA has been severely chastised for talking too much. But such incidents sometimes lead CAs to be overly cautious — too reluctant to communicate with the person and his family. If there are areas that should not be discussed, the CA should frankly say, "This is an area I am not to talk about according to my own personal or professional standards. You must take this up with the person trained to deal with these questions."

People watch very carefully for the reactions of others to their communications. If a family member tells the CA how he feels about his situation or about another person and senses by observing the raise of an eyebrow or a facial grimace that the CA disapproves, this will often set the limit of the communication flow. CAs especially need to be aware of their reactions to others and how others perceive them.

Some interesting norms have developed in the helping professions about the sharing, or rather the nonsharing, of certain kinds of data. In some circles it is considered improper for a CA to express grief, sympathy, or deep concern. It seems that the basic idea is that it seems inappropriate for the CA to wallow in self-pity. But CAs may be able to express real feelings and emotions without giving themselves up to emotions that would not be helpful to others.

The fundamental point here is that problems and situations can be dealt with only to the degree that we know about them. If people are holding back information, the CA cannot really do his job. If they are afraid of the CA, then they will not share all of the data with him. He must build the type of relationship which has enough basic trust that all of the data relevant to the situation can be freely discussed; all feelings, reactions, and concerns can be openly and honestly dealt with. Goals can be set and decisions made only within the realm of the data available.

Goal Setting and Decision Making

In the dependency-building strategy, goals are established by others and imposed on those below them, decisions are made, and the dependency-oriented person abides by the decisions made for him. It would not be surprising to find that in this type of situation there is a low level of commitment to the decisions made and the goals established. A wide range of research data reinforces the principle that commitment to a goal or a decision is directly related to the amount of involvement the people have had in the goal-setting or decision-making process.

In the CA-family relationship, the CA is profoundly concerned with having the person committed to the goal of improving. Often the CA is committed to this goal, but the person is not. When this occurs, the CA often moves to a process of imposed control, trying to coerce, plead, beg, browbeat, threaten, or in some other way force the family member to follow through in the process of improving. One would predict that if the family member is personally committed to the goal of improving he will take the responsibility himself for following proper procedures for his development.

And even within the general process of improving, there is a whole range of decisions that must be made. The model we are examining suggests that the family member and his family should be involved in making these decisions. Again, we often find that the CA has decided that this is good for the family, has really imposed this decision on the individual and the family, and then cannot understand why they don't follow this out. He says to himself, "Don't they know what is good for them?" The answer to this question is often "No, they don't know what is good for them, but they may not be sure that the CA really knows what is best." They may be quite reluctant to follow his program blindly, particularly if there is a somewhat suspicious and nontrusting basic relationship and the CA has communicated very little to them about why he is doing what he is doing.

Some experience in watching the goal-setting, decision-making processes with groups of people suggests that these are not always fixed and immutable operations. Some people like to relook at decisions and reexamine goals, to rethink them and get a new commit-

ment to them. Others like to make the decision once and then move ahead; they cannot understand the former type of person and often become impatient with him. The CA may find all types of persons with whom he works. Some may need to frequently stop and look again at their goals and decisions and really work through the whole process again. Others will make the decision once and move consistently ahead. The CA himself needs to be flexible and allow the family system to follow the best goal-setting, decision-making procedures.

This whole process suggests that the CA must spend time helping the family system (including all involved persons — usually the total family) work through setting goals and making decisions about better family practices. This takes time and is often a bugaboo for the CA who is usually overloaded. It is easier and less time-consuming for the CA to come into the home, appraise the situation, make the decisions, and then tell the family what to do, coming around from time to time to check up and see if they are doing what he has told them. In a real sense, the CA has "taken over." The problem here is that the family is the one that should take over. If the CA is going to terminate the case and feel assured that the family is capable of handling its own situations, then the family unit must take over its own development. When the CA takes over, this is usually the beginning of a dependency relationship or a counterdependency relationship, where the CA has a constant fight on his hands.

Control

This condition has already been alluded to in the previous discussion. The type of control that is used develops out of the three prior conditions. An imposed control system follows almost automatically from the general dependency/counterdependency strategy. We almost have to check up on people and use devices and pressures of various kinds to ensure consistent performance if we are the ones who have made the decisions. McGregor (1960) has suggested that a control strategy really stems from some basic assumptions about people. If we assume that people are basically lazy, stupid, apathetic, irresponsible, then we must make decisions for them, for they are not really capable of making intelligent decisions; then we must follow through and see that they do what we have told them. This strategy and these assumptions are commonly found in parents.

The Gibb model predicts that, if there has developed an authentic, trusting relationship where the family system is free to share all of the data and where the CA has entered into a collaborative relationship with the family goals, then the control problem is basically solved. Self-control is the rather automatic end result of persons or systems having made their own decisions. They are committed to reaching their own goals. If such is the end result of the CA-family interaction, then the dependency problem is in large measure solved. The family system is now not dependent but mature, working *with* the CA.

The Family System

It should be remembered that the whole interaction of the CA is with the family system, not just with one person. The CA is building a relationship with the system, not just with an individual, if he is going to do his best work. All the conditions mentioned apply to the family system. Overlooking this fact may be disastrous. All persons in the system whose behavior is going to be affected by a decision should best be included in the decision-making process.

References

Bradford, Leland P., Jack R. Gibb, and Kenneth D. Benne
  1964 *T-Group Theory and Laboratory Method*. New York: Wiley & Sons, 679–710.

McGregor, Douglas
  1960 *The Human Side of Enterprise*. New York: McGraw-Hill Co.

Parsons, Talcott, and Renee Fox
  1958 Illness, therapy, and the modern urban American family. In *Patients, Physicians and Illness*, ed. G. Jaco. Glencoe: Free Press, 242–43.

ABOUT THE AUTHOR

William G. Dyer is a professor and past chairman of the Organizational Behavior Department at Brigham Young University — currently one of the top-ranked organizational behavior departments in the nation. He holds bachelor's and master's degrees in sociology from BYU and a doctorate in sociology from the University of Wisconsin. During the past twenty years, he has taught at the university level, held various administrative positions, and consulted with over thirty major business firms, church organizations, and government agencies. He has written six books (including *Creating Closer Families: Principles of Positive Family Interaction*, also published by Brigham Young University Press) and more than forty articles. His extensive background in employee- and management-training programs provides the basis for this book, which provides a readable introduction to principles of organizational behavior and business management for college students, professional businessmen, and those who help others develop positive strategies for change.

INDEX